Edmund J. Webb

Africa as Seen by Its Explorers

Edmund J. Webb

Africa as Seen by Its Explorers

ISBN/EAN: 9783337882174

Printed in Europe, USA, Canada, Australia, Japan

Cover: Foto ©Andreas Hilbeck / pixelio.de

More available books at **www.hansebooks.com**

EDITED BY

E. J. WEBB, B.A.

WITH ILLUSTRATIONS

LONDON
EDWARD ARNOLD
37 BEDFORD STREET, STRAND
1899

PREFACE

THE Africa of the explorers is rapidly passing away. Since it was discovered, or even asserted, that money might be made out of regions in which the ambition of our fathers looked to find at the most glory, a new era has set in, when political strife, financial complications, and international rivalries are the themes suggested by the mention of what was, only the other day, considered the Dark Continent. This era, too, will pass away ; but whatever may take its place, the Africa of our ancestors will be gone, the land of mystery and monsters, of strange wild beasts and stranger wild men, which wrought so powerfully upon the imagination of civilized man, from the days of Herodotus down to our own. That the world, whatever it may gain from the new Africa, will lose something in the old, cannot be doubted ; nor will it be denied that the performances of the men who took the leading part in the work of exploration now nearing its end are, upon the whole, among those of which the human race has most reason to be proud. It is hoped that 'Africa as seen by its Explorers' may be of some use in enabling a generation to which such exploits are becoming rare to understand what work its fathers had to do, and how they did it.

An attempt has been made to select such passages as might, when read together, show in some degree what the chief problems of African exploration have been, and by what steps they were gradually solved. As much of this work has been accomplished within the last half-century, extracts from the writings of very many explorers could not be made without the consent of their publishers ; and though this permission has been, in the great majority of cases, accorded with a kindness which must be here gratefully acknowledged, it has in one or two instances been withheld ; which is the reason why no selections have been given from the works of so famous an explorer as David Livingstone. Cordial thanks are due, for permission to print extracts from works of which they are authors or proprietors, to Mr. David Nutt, Mr. Flinders Petrie, Messrs. S. Low and Co., Messrs. W. Blackwood and Sons, the Royal Geographical Society, the Hakluyt Society, Messrs. Longmans and Co., Messrs. Methuen and Co., Sir Frederick Young, K.C.M.G., Mr. E. Stanford, Messrs. G. Philip and Son, Mr. Grant Allen, the *Contemporary Review*, Messrs. Hodder and Stoughton, and Messrs. Smith, Elder and Co.

In preparing these extracts, care has been taken, in every case, to give the exact words of the writer himself or his translator. Where passages have been omitted,

the omission has been marked by asterisks, except in a
few cases where it has amounted to a word or two only.
Very rarely transposition of sentences or paragraphs has
been allowed, as in the extract from Speke, numbered 12.
But no attempt has been made to alter what an author
wrote, even when, as in the case of grammatical blunders,
an alteration might not have displeased him.

In the extracts from the older writers it has been
thought advisable to modernize the spelling to such an
extent as to obviate any possibility of misunderstanding
by inexperienced readers. But no attempt has been
made to adopt a rigorous uniformity of what may pass
for orthography. This would, indeed, be impossible in
the case of proper names, the spelling of which is still so
much a matter of individual taste that it is difficult to
say whether ‘ Morocco ’ or ‘ Marocco ’ is to be considered
the established form of a name familiar in all men's
mouths. Between ‘ pigmy ’ and ‘ pygmy,’ ‘ Tuareg ’ and
‘ Tawárek,’ ‘ Timbuctoo ’ and ‘ Timbuktu,’ posterity,
should it think a decision worth making, must be left
to decide.

CONTENTS

PART I.—EGYPT AND THE NILE.

PART II.—THE GREAT DESERTS AND BORDERING REGIONS.

PART VI.—THE CONGO.

PART VII.—NORTH AFRICA.

PART VIII.—MISCELLANEOUS.

ILLUSTRATIONS

AFRICA

PART I.

EGYPT AND THE NILE.

INTRODUCTION.

THE famous phrase of Herodotus, that Egypt is 'the gift of the river' Nile, has been repeated by almost every traveller. This wonderful land, known from time immemorial as one of the most fruitful regions of the earth, consists of soil brought down and deposited by the great river which, for hundreds of miles, traverses in one narrow thread the vast desert stretching from east to west across the whole of Northern Africa. The rainless land of Egypt depended, not only for its origin, but for its continued existence, on the yearly flood of this river— a river which during the known part of its course received no tributaries, and was never swollen by showers from heaven, but which began to rise always at the hottest season of the year, when all other rivers were falling to their lowest level. It is no wonder that, as soon as men began to please themselves with geographical questions, they should have fixed their attention upon this fascinating question of the Nile, on whose banks had been developed

perhaps the oldest civilization of which mankind re-
members anything.   To the ancient Greeks the antiquity
of Egypt seemed almost as great as it does to us, who
find it difficult to take in that the modern Egyptian
peasant is, as his features (see 6) assure us, the living
descendant of ancestors so remote as those upon whose
great works we look with awe.   And indeed the two
thousand years and more which have elapsed since
Herodotus saw the Pyramids are almost certainly not
so many as those that had passed between the building
of the Pyramids and the time at which Herodotus saw
them.

To behold the sources of the river on which this
civilization, and with it perhaps the civilization of the
whole world, had arisen, was a noble ambition, which
many ages have felt, and all of them, until our own age,
in vain.   As in the first century of the Christian era
Lucan, the Roman poet, to whom Bruce (see 9) refers,
addressed the Nile as the river on whose cradle the
nations were not privileged to look, so to an English
poet of the nineteenth century it was still

> ' That Egyptian tide whose birth
> Is hidden from the sons of earth.'

The following extracts are designed to show in some
measure by what steps and with what labour the secret
has been revealed, since the old-world fancies reported by
Herodotus gave way to the scientific conceptions of later
antiquity such as appear in Strabo.   How far Greeks
or Romans went up the river is uncertain, but a curious
passage from Seneca (10) is regarded as strong evidence
that one expedition must have reached the ' sudd,' or
great grass - block, on the White Nile, which has so
seriously impeded modern travellers.   But the summary

of early information about the Nile sources is contained in a famous passage from the Geography of Ptolemy (quoted 16), who makes the river flow from two lakes, which are fed by snows from a mountain-range. From his time down to the middle of the nineteenth century these mysterious Mountains of the Moon used to occupy a prominent position—by no means always the same position—on the maps of Africa. But until that time no certain news either of them or of the lakes was obtained by man.

In the latter part of the eighteenth century, indeed, a great stir was made by the exploit of the celebrated traveller, Bruce, who, starting from the Red Sea, found his way to the sources of the Blue Nile in Abyssinia, and prided himself not a little on having solved the question to which the world had so long been seeking an answer. But a short time sufficed to show that, as Bruce himself might have noticed on his descent of the stream to Egypt (see 15), the Blue Nile had no right whatever to be considered the main branch of the river. And, while exploration worked its way but slowly up the stream of the White Nile — navigable only with difficulty, and beset by savage tribes—the first proof that great lakes, vast reservoirs of the Nile, do really exist was obtained by travellers coming overland from the west coast at Zanzibar.

It is true that the lake first reached by Burton and Speke, the beautiful Tanganyika (see 83), has no connection with the Nile. But Speke, pushing on alone, discovered, to the north.of Tanganyika and at a much higher level, the lake Victoria Nyanza, the waters of which stretched so far to the north that it was clear they must reach to within a few hundred miles of the region through which the upper Nile had already been

proved to flow. On a second journey he succeeded in
working his way round the lake and reaching the spot—
now known as Ripon Falls—where the waters of the
lake escaped to the north in the form of a river. There
could now be no doubt that he had found if not *the*
source yet *a* source of the Nile.

In descending towards the north, Speke and his companion were compelled for a time to leave the newly-
found river, which flowed away to the west. When
they regained it, they met Mr. Baker coming up the
stream; and he, continuing his course, discovered the
second great lake—Albert Nyanza—into which the river
they had left flowed, almost immediately to emerge again.
It was for some time doubted whether this second lake
could properly be considered as a separate reservoir of
the Nile, as it might be a kind of backwater, fed only by
the river descending from the Victoria Nyanza. But it
is now known that this is not the case, since the Albert
receives a large river from another and higher lake, the
so-called Albert Edward Nyanza.

Thus were the long-sought lakes of the Nile discovered
at last—true sources of the great river, though not its
only sources, for the mighty body of water brought into
it from the west by the Bahr-al-Ghazal, or Gazelle River
(see 15), owes nothing to them. But what of the
Mountains of the Moon?

Mountains enough Bruce found at the Abyssinian
sources, but he was obliged to admit that they were
not snow-covered. Burton, too, pointed out that the
modern name — Unyamwezi — of the country to the
south of the Victoria Nyanza actually meant 'the land
of the moon'; and Speke had no difficulty in fixing on
the particular hills to which the old name might have
been applied. But none of these had snow upon them;

and those who thought Ptolemy had reason for his words
—and, indeed, it was unlikely he would without good
reason place snow-clad mountains in an equatorial region
—supposed that he might have heard of the great eastern
mountains, Kenia and Kilimanjaro (see 84), and wrongly
concluded that they supplied rivers to the Nile lakes.
But on his last great journey Mr. Stanley made the
unexpected discovery that a huge snow-covered mountain
—now known to us as Ruwenzori—does actually exist in
the region of the Nile sources, and sends its melted snows
to feed the lakes from which the ancient river takes
its rise.

1. THE SOURCE OF THE NILE.

HERODOTUS,* B.C. 450.

As touching the nature of the river Nilus, I could not
be satisfied either by the priests, or by any other, being
always very willing and desirous to hear something
thereof first, what the cause might be that growing to
so great increase, it should drown and overgo the whole
country, beginning to swell the eighth day before the
Kalends of July, and continuing in flood a hundred days,
after which time, in the like number of days it falleth
again, flowing within the compass of its own bank till
the next approach of July.

Of the causes of these things the people of Egypt
were ignorant themselves, not able to tell me anything,
whether Nilus had any proper and peculiar virtue
different from the nature of other floods. About which
matters being very inquisitive, moved with desire of

* Englished by B. R., 1584; edited by A. Lang. (David Nutt,
1888.)

knowledge, I demanded moreover the reason and occasion why this stream of all others never sent forth any mist or vapour, such as are commonly seen to ascend and rise from the waters ; but herein also I was fain to nestle in mine own ignorance, desiring to be led of those that were as blind as myself. Howbeit, certain Grecian writers thinking to purchase the price and praise of wit, have gone about to discourse of Nilus and set down their judgment of the nature thereof, who are found to vary and dissent in three sundry opinions, two of the which I suppose not worth the naming, but only to give the reader intelligence how ridiculous they are.

The first is that the overflow of Nilus cometh of none other cause than that the winds, Etesiæ so named, blowing directly upon the stream thereof, hinder and beat back the waters from flowing into the sea, which winds are commonly wont to arise, and have their season a long time after the increase and rising of the Nilus ; but imagine it were otherwise, yet this of necessity must follow, that all rivers whatsoever having a full and direct course against the winds Etesiæ, shall in like manner swell and grow over their banks, and so much the rather by how much the less and weak the floods themselves are whose streams are opposed against the same. But there be many rivers as well in Syria as in Africa that suffer no such motion and change as hath been said of the flood Nilus. There is another opinion, of less credit and learning, albeit of greater wonder and admiration than the first, alleging the cause of the rising to be, for that the river (say they) proceedeth from the Ocean sea, which environeth the whole globe and circle of the earth.

The third opinion being more calm and modest than the rest, is also more false and unlikely than them both, affirming that the increase and augmentation of Nilus comes of the snow waters molten and thawed in those regions, carrying with it so much the less credit and authority, by how much the more it is evident that the river coming from Africa through the midst of Ethiopia, runs continually from the hotter countries to the colder, being in no wise probable, or anything likely that the waxing of the waters should proceed of snow. Many sound proofs may be brought to the weakening of this cause, whereby we may guess how grossly they err which think so great a stream to be increased by snow. What greater reason may be found to the contrary than that the winds blowing from those countries are very warm by nature? Moreover, the land itself is continually void of rain and ice, being most necessary that within five days after the fall of snow there should come rain, whereby it cometh to pass that if it snow in Egypt, it must also of necessity rain. The same is confirmed and established by the blackness and swartness of the people, coloured by the vehement heat and scorching of the sun; likewise by the swallows and kites which continually keep in those coasts; lastly, by the flight of the cranes toward the coming of winter, which are always wont to fly out of Scythia and the cold regions to these places, where all the winter season they make their abode.

Were it then that never so little snow could fall in those countries by the which Nilus hath his course, and from which he stretcheth his head and beginning, it were not possible for any of these things to happen which experience proveth to be true. They which talk of Oceanus, grounding their judgment upon a mere fable, want reason to prove it. For I think there is no such sea as Ocean, but rather that Homer or some one of the ancient poets devised the name, and made use thereof afterwards in their tales and poetry.

     *   *   *   *   *

But let these things be as they are, and have been always.

The head and fountain of Nilus where it is, or from whence it cometh, none of the Egyptians, Grecians, or Africans that ever I talked with could tell me anything, besides a certain scribe of Minerva's treasury in the city Sais, who seemed to me to speak merrily, saying that undoubtedly he knew the place, describing the same in this manner. There be two mountains (quoth he) arising into sharp and spindled tops, situate between Syêne, a city of Thebais and Elephantina, the one called Crophi, the other Mophi. From the vale between the two hills doth issue out the head of the river Nilus, being of an unsearchable depth, and without bottom, half of the water running towards Egypt and the north, the other half towards Ethiopia and the south. Of the immeasurable depth of the fountain the scribe affirmed that Psammetichus, King of the Egyptians, had taken trial, who, sounding the waters with a rope of many miles in length, was unable to feel any ground or bottom ; whose tale (if any such thing were done as he said) made me think that in those places whereof he spake were ce tain gulfs or whirlpools, very swift, violent, and raging, which by reason of the fall of the water from the hills would not suffer the line with the sounding lead to sink to the bottom, for which cause they were supposed to be bottomless.

Besides this, I could learn nothing of any man. Nevertheless, travelling to Elephantina to behold the thing with mine own eyes, and making diligent inquiry to know the truth, I understood this : that taking our journey from thence southward to the countries above, at length we shall come to a steep and bending shelf, where the river falleth with great violence, so that we must be forced to fasten two cables to each side of the ship, and in that sort to hale and draw her forward, which if they chance either to slip or break, the vessel is by-and-by driven backwards by the intolerable rage and violence of the waters.

2. THE NILE FLOOD.

STRABO, THE GREEK GEOGRAPHER, A.D. I.

Of such excellence is the management of the river that industry here prevails over nature. For nature indeed makes the land yield abundantly, but irrigation more abundantly still; and whereas, in the natural course of things, the higher the flood, the larger is the region irrigated, often when nature has failed industry has succeeded in irrigating as much land at a lesser flood as at a greater, by means of ditches and embankments. In the days before Petronius the greatest yield came with the greatest flood, when the Nile rose fourteen cubits; and if it rose only eight it brought famine with it. But under his administration of the country the yield was at its greatest even when twelve cubits only were registered, and if no more than eight were registered, yet no famine was experienced. . . .

From the borders of Ethiopia the Nile flows in a straight line northward to the region known as the Delta. . . . This is an island enclosed by the sea and the two branches of the river, and it is called Delta (Δ) because of its resemblance in shape. . . . At the risings of the Nile it is all overflowed, and appears, but for the habitations of men, like a sea, which habitations, important towns and villages alike, are built upon natural hillocks or artificial mounds, and seen from afar wear the appearance of islands. The water continues for more than forty days of summer, and then goes down gradually as it rose, until in sixty days the plain is completely laid bare and dried. The more quickly it dries, the sooner it is ploughed and sown, and it dries the more quickly where the heat is the greatest.

Above the Delta the country is irrigated in the same way, saving only that here, for some 4,000 stades in a straight line, the river flows in one channel, except where interrupted by some island, or diverted by some canal into a large lake or district capable of irrigation. But speaking generally, the Egypt of the river-valley is no more than the strip of country lying on each bank of the Nile, and from the borders of Ethiopia to the apex of the Delta rarely comprises an unbroken breadth of habitable land to the extent of 300 stades across. It is therefore, if we disregard the frequent diversions of the stream, like a ribbon stretched out lengthwise. This configuration of the valley and the country generally is due to the mountains which run down from the neighbourhood of Syene [Assuan] to the Egyptian Sea ; for in proportion as they approach or recede from each other, so is the river contracted or spread out, and gives a different shape to the habitable region. For beyond the mountains the country is in great measure uninhabited.

Both ancients and moderns, the former for the most part by guess-work, but the latter from the evidence of their own eyes, have concluded that the Nile is swollen when Upper Ethiopia, especially in its remotest mountains, is drenched by summer rains, and that when the rains have ceased the flood by degrees ceases too. This was most plainly perceived by those who navigated the Arabian Gulf as far as the cinnamon country, and by those who were sent out to catch elephants, or with any of the other objects which induced the Ptolemaic kings of Egypt to despatch men to those parts. For those kings took great interest in such matters ; above all, he that was surnamed Philadelphus, who loved scientific inquiry, and on account of his weak health was always craving after some new study or amusement. But the kings of old took no great interest in these things, although they, too, were students of philosophy ; and not only they, but the priests with whom they passed most of their lives. For which reason, and also because Sesostris traversed the whole of Ethiopia up to the cinnamon country, leaving memorials of his expedition in the shape of pillars and inscriptions which are still shown, while Cambyses, during his occupation of Egypt, penetrated with a retinue of Egyptians as far as Meroe, it is surprising that the truth about the rains should not have been clearly known to the men of those times. . . .

Syene and Elephantine are, the one a town upon the frontier of Egypt and Ethiopia, the other an island in the Nile, lying half a stade in advance of Syene, with a town upon it, in which are a temple of Cnuph and a Nilometer, as at Memphis. The Nilometer is a well upon the bank of the Nile, constructed out of stones shaped to fit into each other, by which, on the principle that the water in the well rises and falls with the river, they register the risings of the Nile as very high, or very low, or of average height. There are, of course, marks at the side upon the walls of the well to show the extent of the floods—whether they attain the full height or fall short of it in any degree ; and by observing these marks they can send information to the rest of the world ; for by these signs they know long beforehand what the coming flood will be, and announce it. And by this not only the farmers profit, in respect of the storing of water, embankments, trenches, and the like, but the Government too in respect of the revenue ; for the higher the flood, the higher the revenue it foretells.

3. THE NILE FLOOD.

SIR ALFRED MILNER,* 1892.

Egypt, as a geographical expression, is two things—the Desert and the Nile. As a habitable country, it is only one—the Nile. Every square foot of cultivable land has, at some time or other, been brought down by the river which now flows in its midst—at one season a shallow and sluggish stream, of which but little reaches the sea ; at another, a sea itself, here spreading in a vast lake over the whole face of the country, there pouring along through numerous channels towards the ocean, and filling the remotest corners of the land with the rush and the sound of many waters.

The ordinary visitor to Egypt knows nothing of these things. He goes up the Nile ; but, as far as the stream itself is concerned, he is almost invariably disappointed. Passing over the bridge at Cairo, he looks down upon the most remarkable river in the world, a river with which no other can compare in the strangeness of its character, the richness of its gifts, the immense *rôle* it has played in human history. But it makes no more impression on him than the Thames at London Bridge. The breadth of the stream is not remarkable—about a

* ' England in Egypt.' (Edward Arnold.)

quarter of a mile; the volume of water is not great; the colour is dull; the pace of the current is, if anything, slow. Yet the Nile, as the tourist sees it, from December to March, is full and strong and stately compared to what it afterwards becomes.

In April, May, and June, and sometimes into the beginning of July, the water at Cairo falls and falls. The lowering of level would be even more marked if the Nile were not nowadays pounded up at the Barrage, some fourteen miles further down, in order to feed the summer canals which keep the cultivation of the Delta alive. Meantime the two branches of the river below the Barrage are almost dry. There are many points at which, during the season of low water, a child might walk across. The fields, except where artificially nourished by the careful doling out of water from the canals, are parched and seamed with fissures. The air is full of dust. The brilliant green of the crops, which so strikes the visitor during the winter, has given way to more sombre hues. The trees have shed their leaves. Nor is the animal world less oppressed by the lack of water. Man and beast alike languish. And all day long the fiery sun, undimmed by the lightest cloud, proceeds on his stately but pitiless march through a sky of deepest blue, as if determined to dry up what still remains of life-giving moisture, and to restore the tiny strip of cultivated Egypt to the vast surrounding desert, in which, for hundreds of miles, it forms the only break.

Towards the end of the dry season the physical distress of the people becomes great and visible. And that physical distress is heightened by mental anxiety as to how long this tyranny will continue. The level of the water is still sinking. Already some of the least valuable crops have had to be given up; the more valuable ones are threatened.   High and low, rich and poor are united in one common solicitude.   What is the news from Assuan ?* Has the river risen ?   Is it not later than usual ?   Does it not look like a bad year ?   Will it ever rise sufficiently to save the cotton ?   One day a message of hope is flashed over Egypt.   There is a rise of some inches at Assuan. The next day there is again a rise.   From one end of the country. to the other the countenances of men show signs of relief.   But their joy is premature.   The next day the ver has gone down again.   It was a false rise, the pre- cursor, as so often happens, of the real flood.   Such alternations of hope and disappointment frequently con- tinue for a week or a fortnight before the true rise unmistakably begins.

At the commencement of the flood it takes ten or twelve days before a rise at Assuan makes itself felt at Cairo. When that time has elapsed, anyone watching on the river bank at the latter place may note how, from day to day, at first slowly, then with ever-increasing rapidity, the water creeps up the bank.   After the first week or two, it is no longer only the level, but the whole demeanour of the river, which shows signs of the coming change. Gradually, surely, the current quickens, the water assumes a deeper colour.   During the low season, a bather in the Nile may easily make headway against the current.   In the first eight days of the descending flood he may still swim up-stream, though with increasing difficulty. Another eight days, and all his efforts will only keep him

* Of course, the earliest news of the state of the Nile comes, not from Assuan, but from the frontier at Halfa, as, before the loss of the Sudan. it came from Khartum.   The engineers go by the reports from Halfa.   But what the mass of the people, by immemorial habit, are accustomed to look to, is the height of the river at Assuan—the boundary of Egypt proper.   The meaning of so many ' pics ' (cubits) of water at Assuan is understood by every peasant in Egypt.

stationary. Eight days more, and all swimming is impossible. By the middle of August the river has risen
some twenty feet, and nears the summit of its banks.
Its discharge has increased from thirty millions of cubic
metres a day to six hundred millions.* Cross the bridge
at night—in one of those balmy Egyptian nights which
are unequalled for their purity and their brilliance—and
listen to the great river, which six weeks before hardly
made its presence felt—so low down was it, so sluggish,
and so noiseless—but which now swirls and roars about
the piers, as if it would sweep everything before it!
There are few more striking manifestations of the might
of Nature. And the impression is heightened by the fact
that, for months past, not a drop of rain has fallen. No
cloud has crossed the sky. There has been no sign of
storm or thunder. It is to the tropical rains of countries
1,500 and 2,000 miles off that this tumult of waters
is due.

And now the basins of Upper Egypt are rapidly filling
with water. By the middle of September, as you stand
on one of the low desert hills and look over the country,
it is all a huge lake, while in the Delta both branches of
the Nile and the numberless artificial channels are flowing
at full speed. The whole land is a land of rivers, as erst-
while it was a land of dust. Physical comfort is restored.
The spirits of men have risen as the waters rose. Crops,
cattle, human beings, all rejoice together in the abundance
of the first necessary of life. The water, charged as it
is with quantities of fine mud, is murky to look at, but

---

* The average daily discharge of the Nile at Cairo in the flood
months — which are, roughly speaking, August, September, and
October—is upwards of six hundred million cubic metres. In the
lowest years it has been as little as four hundred and fifty millions;
in the highest it has sometimes exceeded one thousand millions.

it is refreshing to bathe in and wholesome to drink. Wherever you go on the banks of the canals, you see brown-skinned men and boys plunging with delight into the life-giving stream. Women are drawing from it, dogs are lapping it, the great patient buffaloes are standing up to their necks in it, pictures of content.

4. THE PYRAMIDS.

W. FLINDERS PETRIE.*

The small piece of desert plateau opposite the village of Gizeh, though less than a mile across, may well claim to be the most remarkable piece of ground in the world. There may be seen the very beginning of architecture, the most enormous piles of building ever raised, the most accurate constructions known, the finest masonry, and the employment of the most ingenious tools, whilst among all the sculpture that we know, the largest figure—the Sphinx—and also the finest example of technical skill with artistic expression—the Statue of Khafra—both belong to Gizeh. We shall look in vain for a more wonderful assemblage than the vast masses of the Pyramids, the ruddy walls and pillars of the granite temple, the titanic head of the Sphinx, the hundreds of tombs, and the shattered outlines of causeways, pavements, and walls, that cover this earliest field of man's labours.

But these remains have an additional, though passing, interest in the present day, owing to the many attempts that have been made to theorise on the motives of their origin and construction. The Great Pyramid has lent its name as a sort of byword for paradoxes; and, as

* ' Pyramids and Temples of Gizeh.' (Field and Tuer, 1885.)

moths to a candle, so are theorisers attracted to it. The
very fact that the subject was so generally familiar, and
yet so little was actually known about it, made it the
more enticing ; there were plenty of descriptions from
which to choose, and yet most of them were so hazy
that their support could be claimed for many varying
theories. Here, then, was a field which called for the
resources of the present time for its due investigation ;
a field in which measurement and research were greatly
needed, and have now been largely rewarded by the
disclosures of the skill of the ancients and the mistakes
of the moderns.

5. THE PYRAMIDS.

E. D. CLARKE.* 1812.

We were roused, as soon as the sun dawned, by Antony,
our faithful Greek servant and interpreter, with the intelligence that the Pyramids were in view. We hastened
from the cabin ; and never will the impression made
by their appearance be obliterated. By reflecting the
sun's rays, they appeared as white as snow, and of such
surprising magnitude, that nothing we had previously
conceived in our imagination had prepared us for the
spectacle we beheld.

The sight instantly convinced us that no power of
description, no delineation, can convey ideas adequate to
the effect produced in viewing these stupendous monuments. The formality of their structure is lost in their
prodigious magnitude ; the mind, elevated by wonder,
feels at once the force of an axiom which, however dis-
puted, experience confirms, that in vastness, whatsoever
be its nature, there dwells sublimity.

* 'Travels in Various Countries. (London, 1814.)

Another proof of their indescribable power is, that no one ever approached them under other emotions than those of terror, which is another principal source of the sublime.   In certain instances of irritable feeling, this impression of awe and fear has been so great as to cause pain rather than pleasure. . . .   Hence, perhaps, have originated descriptions of the Pyramids which represent them as deformed and gloomy masses, without taste or beauty.   Persons who have derived no satisfaction from the contemplation of them may not have been conscious that the uneasiness they experienced was a result of their own sensibility.   Others have acknowledged ideas widely different, excited by every wonderful circumstance of character and of situation ; ideas of duration, almost endless ; of power, inconceivable ; of majesty, supreme ; of solitude, most awful ; of grandeur, of desolation, and of repose.

*   *   *   *   *

In the observations of travellers who had recently preceded us, we had heard the Pyramids described as huge objects which gave no satisfaction to the spectator on account of their barbarous shape and formal appearance ; yet to us it appeared hardly possible that persons susceptible of any feeling of sublimity could behold them unmoved.   With what amazement did we survey the vast surface that was presented to us when we arrived at this stupendous monument which seemed to reach the clouds!   Here and there appeared some Arab guides upon the immense masses above us, like so many pigmies waiting to show the way up to the summit.   Now and then we thought we heard voices and listened, but it was the wind, in powerful gusts, sweeping the immense ranges of stone. . . .

The mode of ascent has been frequently described,

and yet, from the questions which are often proposed to
travellers, it does not appear to be generally understood.
The reader may imagine himself to be upon a staircase,
every step of which, to a man of middle stature, is nearly
breast high ; and the breadth of each step is equal to its
height, consequently, the footing is secure ; and although
a retrospect in going up be sometimes fearful to persons
unaccustomed to look down from any considerable elevation, yet there is little danger of falling. . . . At length
we reached the topmost tier, to the great delight and
satisfaction of all the party. Here we found a platform
32 feet square, consisting of nine large stones, each
of which might weigh about a ton, although they be
much inferior in size to some of the stones used in the
construction of this Pyramid.

The view from this eminence amply fulfilled our
expectations, nor do the accounts which have been given
of it as it appears at this season of the year exaggerate
the novelty and grandeur of the sight. All the region
towards Cairo and the Delta resembled a sea, covered
with innumerable islands. Forests of palm-trees were
seen standing in the water, the inundation spreading over
the land where they stood, so as to give them an appearance of growing in the flood. To the north, as far as
the eye could reach, nothing could be discerned but a
watery surface thus diversified by plantations and by
villages. To the south we saw the Pyramids of Saccára,
and, upon the east of these, smaller monuments of the
same kind nearer to the Nile. An appearance of
ruins might, indeed, be traced the whole way from
the Pyramids of Djiza to those of Saccára, as if they
had been once connected so as to constitute one vast
cemetery.

Beyond the Pyramids of Saccára we could perceive

the distant mountains of the Saïd; and upon an eminence, near the Libyan side of the Nile, appeared a monastery of considerable size. Towards the west and south-west the eye ranged over the great Libyan Desert, extending to the utmost verge of the horizon, without a single object to interrupt the dreary horror of the landscape, except dark, floating spots caused by the shadows of passing clouds upon the sand.

    *   *   *   *   *

It is impossible to leave the Pyramids of Djiza without some notice of the long list of philosophers, marshals, emperors, and princes, who, in so many ages, have been brought to view the most wonderful of the works of man. There has not been a conqueror pre-eminently distinguished in the history of the world, from the days of Cambyses down to the invasion of Napoleon Buonaparte, who withheld the tribute of his admiration from the genius of the place. The vanity of Alexander the Great was so piqued by the overwhelming impression of their majesty, that nothing less than being ranked among the gods of Egypt could elevate him sufficiently above the pride of the monarchs by whom they were erected. When Germanicus had subdued the Egyptian Empire, and seated 'a Roman præfect upon the splendid throne of the Ptolemies,' being unmindful of repose or of triumph, the antiquities of the country engaged all his attention.

The humblest pilgrim, pacing the Libyan sands around them, while he is conscious that he walks in the footsteps of so many mighty and renowned men, imagines himself to be for an instant admitted into their illustrious conclave. Persian satraps, Macedonian heroes, Grecian bards, sages, and historians, Roman warriors, all of every age, nation, and religion, have participated, in

common with him, the same feelings, and have trodden the same ground. Every spot that he beholds, every stone on which he rests his weary limbs, have witnessed the coming of men who were the fathers of law, of literature, and of the arts. . . .

6. THE SPHYNX.

A. W. KINGLAKE.*

And near the Pyramids, more wondrous, and more awful than all else in the land of Egypt, there sits the lonely Sphynx. Comely the creature is, but the comeliness is not of this world; the once-worshipped beast is a deformity and a monster to this generation, and yet you can see that those lips, so thick and heavy, were fashioned according to some ancient mould of beauty—some mould of beauty now forgotten—forgotten because that Greece drew forth Cytherea from the flashing foam of the Ægean, and in her image created new forms of beauty, and made it a law among men that the short and proudly-wreathed lip should stand for the sign and the main condition of loveliness through all generations to come. Yet still there lives on the race of those who were beautiful in the fashion of the elder world, and Christian girls of Coptic blood will look on you with the sad, serious gaze, and kiss your charitable hand with the big pouting lips of the very Sphynx.

Laugh and mock if you will at the worship of stone idols, but mark ye this, ye breakers of images, that in one regard, the stone idol bears awful semblance of Deity—unchangefulness in the midst of change—the same seeming will and intent for ever and ever inexor-

* 'Eothen,' 1850.

able! Upon ancient dynasties of Ethiopian and Egyptian
kings, upon Greek and Roman, upon Arab and Ottoman
conquerors, upon Napoleon dreaming of an Eastern
Empire, upon battle and pestilence, upon the ceaseless
misery of the Egyptian race, upon keen-eyed travellers
—Herodotus yesterday, and Warburton to-day—upon
all and more this unworldly Sphynx has watched and
watched like a Providence with the same earnest eyes,
and the same sad, tranquil mien. And we, we shall die,
and Islam will wither away, and the Englishman, straining far over to hold his loved India, will plant a firm
foot on the banks of the Nile, and sit in the seats of the
Faithful, and still that sleepless rock will lie watching
and watching the works of the new busy race with those
same sad, earnest eyes, and the same tranquil mien everlasting. You dare not mock at the Sphynx.

7. THE FASCINATION OF THE NILE.

COLONEL SIR W. F. BUTLER.[*]

For more than two months I had lived on the river,
and it was no wonder that, knowing it in its every phase
of light and darkness, one had come to feel a good deal
of that strange companionship which the Nile has ever
exercised over the minds of those who dwell upon its
shores or sail its waters. What the secret of that friendship is it would not be easy to define, but its presence
has too often been attested to allow even this age, which
makes the whole world too small for man, to doubt its
reality.

I do not think that secret is to be found in the memory
of the bygone glory of the river, nor in the ruins which

[*] 'Campaign of the Cataracts.' (S. Low and Co., 1887.)

still stand to verify, even in their desolation, history which, without them, would read as fable, nor in the contrast between man's misery to-day and his magnificence in the past. These, and more than these memories grow thicker than palm or mimosa on the shores, but they are sad as Nubia's twilight hour, which nowhere sinks upon the earth in light and shadow more intensely mournful. Nor yet do I think that this secret charm is to be looked for in the contrast ever in sight between river and desert, between the extreme of the dry and barren, and the border of green which, though a fringe, is rich with the colour carried from a thousand tropic sources ; but those who dwell upon the Nile literally live upon it ; it is life ; all else—the desert, the cloudless, rainless sky, the pitiless sun, the blighting breath of the simoom—these are death, death with torment of thirst and hunger ; but here, centred in a single stream, is every gift that shower, shade, and sun yield to man on the most favoured regions of the earth.

It is this sole principle of life made ever present through every sense that gives the Nile the power of tying to it the hopes, wants, and thoughts of its people, making the river that one central point of home which in other lands is diffused over many objects. You will find the modern Nubian working on the wharves of Alexandria and in the streets of Cairo, but his toil and his service have only one object—to get back again to that fringe of life amid the sea of death which is his home. There, until the Turk came, he was probably the happiest peasant on the globe. The brown water was better than the clearest spring to him. The steep shelving bank of clayey sand was his garden, where it rose curving into contours formed by successive water-levels, bright with green-leaved ' lubia ' and sweet-blossoming beans, where the summer flood had softened and fertilized the soil. Higher up, the mimosa, green of leaf and yellow of flower, scented the air with the perfume its deep roots drew from the water. The ringdove cooed deep amid the branches, and big black-and-yellow bees were thick around the blossoms. Beyond the mimosa came the palm group, where the north wind rustled cool in the mid-day, and the shade was flecked with sunshine.

Beyond the palms the dhurra stood, tall and ripe in November, or the wheat was green in January, both drawing their life from the 'sakeeyeh' channel, whose rill the oxen in their ceaseless round kept ever flowing. Beyond all, the grim face of the desert looked down upon his little oasis, a wall of rock to him in life, a grave of sand to him in death.

8. THE MEETING OF THE WATERS AT KHARTUM.

Dr. R. LEPSIUS.[*]

The same evening we arrived at Chartûm. This name signified 'elephant's trunk,' and is probably derived from the narrow tongue of land between its Niles, on which the city lies.

* * * * *

A day or two after I took a walk . . . to the opposite side of the promontory, toward the White River, which we followed to its union with the Blue River. Its water is, in fact, whiter, and tastes less agreeably than that of the Blue, because it runs slowly through several lakes in the upper countries, the standing waters of which lakes impart to it an earthy and impure taste. I have filled

---

[*] ' Discoveries in Egypt.' (Bentley, 1852.)

several bottles with the water of the Blue and the White
Nile, which I shall bring home sealed down.

*   *   *   *   *

We went up the White River on the fourteenth ; but
soon returned, as it has so weak a current that, by the
present prevailing north wind, the way back is somewhat
difficult. The shores of the White River are desolate,
and the few trees which formerly stood in the vicinity
of Chartûm are now cut down and used for building or
burning. The water mass of the White River is greater
than that of the Blue, and retains its direction after their
union ; so the Blue River is to be looked upon rather
as a tributary, but the White River as the actual Nile.
Their different waters may be distinguished long after
their juncture.

9. THE SOURCES OF THE BLUE NILE.

J. BRUCE,* 1770.

This triple ridge of mountains disposed one range
behind the other, nearly in form of three concentric
circles, seem to suggest an idea that they are the Mountains of the Moon, or the *Montes Lunæ* of antiquity, at the
foot of which the Nile was said to rise ; in fact, there are
no others. . . . The hail lies often upon the top of Amid
Amid for hours ; but snow was never seen in this country,
nor have they a word in their language for it. . . .

At three quarters after one we arrived at the top of
the mountain, whence we had a distinct view of all the
remaining territory of Sacala, the mountain Geesh, and
church of St. Michael Geesh, about a mile and a half
distant from St. Michael Sacala, where we then were.

* 'Travels to Discover the Source of the Nile.'

We saw, immediately below us, the Nile itself, strangely
diminished in size, and now only a brook that had scarcely
water to turn a mill.   I could not satiate myself with the
sight, revolving in my mind all those classical prophecies
that had given the Nile up to perpetual obscurity and
concealment.   The lines of the poet came immediately
into my mind, and I enjoyed here, for the first time, the
triumph which already, by the protection of Providence
and my own intrepidity, I had gained over all that were
powerful, and all that were learned, since the remotest
antiquity. . . .

The Nile here is not four yards over, and not above
four inches deep where we crossed ; it was indeed become
a very trifling brook, but ran swiftly over a bottom of
small stones, with hard, black rock appearing amidst
them ; it is at this place very easy to pass, and very
limpid, but, a little lower, full of inconsiderable falls ;
the ground rises gently from the river to the southward,
full of small hills and eminences, which you ascend and
descend almost imperceptibly.   The whole company had
halted on the north side of St. Michael's Church, and
there I reached them without affecting any hurry.

     *   *   *   *   *

' Come, come,' said I ; ' we understand each other.   No
more words ; it is now late.   Lose no more time, but
carry me to Geesh and the head of the Nile directly
without preamble, and show me the hill that separates
me from it.'   He then carried me round to the south side
of the church, out of the grove of trees that surrounded
it.   ' This is the hill,' says he, looking archly, ' that, when
you was on the other side of it, was between you and the
fountains of the Nile ; there is no other.   Look at that
hillock of green sod in the middle of that watery spot ;
it is in that the two fountains of the Nile are to be found.

Geesh is on the face of the rock where yon green trees are ; if you go the length of the fountains, pull off your shoes as you did the other day, for these people are all Pagans, worse than those that were at the ford ; and they believe in nothing that you believe, but only in this river, to which they pray every day as if it were God ; but this perhaps you may do likewise.'

Half undressed as I was by loss of my sash, and throwing my shoes off, I ran down the hill towards the little island of green sods, which was about 200 yards distant ; the whole side of the hill was thick grown over with flowers, the large bulbous roots of which appearing above the surface of the ground, and their skins coming off on treading upon them, occasioned two very severe falls before I reached the brink of the marsh. I after this came to the island of green turf, which was in form of an altar, apparently the work of art, and I stood in rapture over the principal fountain which rises in the middle of it.

It is easier to guess than to describe the situation of my mind at that moment—standing in that spot which had baffled the genius, industry, and inquiry of both ancients and moderns for the course of near 3,000 years. Kings had attempted this discovery at the head of armies, and each expedition was distinguished from the last only by the difference of the numbers which had perished, and agreed alone in the disappointment which had uniformly, and without exception, followed them all. Fame, riches, and honour had been held out for a series of ages to every individual of those myriads these princes commanded without having produced one man capable of gratifying the curiosity of his sovereign, or wiping off this stain upon the enterprise and abilities of mankind, or adding this desideratum for the encouragement of

geography.   Though a mere private Briton, I triumphed
here, in my own mind, over kings and their armies ; and
every comparison was leading nearer and nearer to pre-
sumption when the place itself where I stood—the object
of my vain-glory—suggested what depressed my short-
lived triumphs.   I was but a few minutes arrived at the
sources of the Nile, through numberless dangers and
sufferings, the least of which would have overwhelmed
me but for the continual goodness and protection of
Providence ; I was, however, but then half through my
journey, and all those dangers which I had already passed
awaited me again on my return.   I found a despondency
gaining ground fast upon me, and blasting the crown of
laurels I had too rashly woven for myself.

10. THE 'SUDD' ON THE WHITE NILE.

SENECA,* A.D. 55.

I myself have heard the two centurions whom, in his
zeal for truth, as for all other virtues, Nero Cæsar sent
forth to explore the sources of the Nile, relate how they
reached the interior and made therein a long journey,
furnished with supplies from the King of Ethiopia, and
by him commended to the neighbouring princes.

' We came,' they said, ' to a remote region, to immense
marshes, the outlet from which neither the natives knew,
nor could anyone hope to attain to it, so mingled were
grasses with the water, and the water impassable to men
travelling either on foot or with a boat, seeing that a
small kind, holding one person only, was as much as the
muddy and tangled marsh could sustain.'

* ' Naturales Quaestiones.'

11. THE SUDD.

DR. SCHWEINFURTH.[*] 1869.

The hindrances to our progress caused by the excessive vegetation began now to give us some anxiety. All day long we were bewildered, not only by the multiplicity of channels, but by masses of grass, papyrus, and ambatch, which covered the whole stream like a carpet, and even when they opened gave merely the semblance of being passages. It is quite possible that the diversion of its course to the east, which for sixty miles the Nile here takes, may check the progress of the stream, and be in a measure the cause of such a strange accumulation of water-plants. Certain it seems that neither any exceptional depth of water, such as may occur in particular years, nor yet any general overflow wider than usual, avails to exercise the slightest influence upon this exuberant vegetation.

Were it a coating of ice it would split itself into fragments under the pressure of the stream, but here is a real web of tough tangle, which blockades the entire surface. Every here and there, indeed, the force of the water may open a kind of rift, but not corresponding at all with the deeper and true channel of the stream. Such a rift is not available for any passage of the boats. The strain of the tension, which goes on without intermission, has such an effect in altering the position of the weedy mass, that even the most experienced pilot is at a loss how to steer, consequently every voyage in winter is along a new course, and through a fresh labyrinth of tangle. But in July, when the floods are at their highest, navigation can be carried on along well-nigh all the channels, since the

---

[*] 'The Heart of Africa.' (S. Low and Co., 1873.)

currents are not so strong, and the vessels are able to proceed without detention to their destinations.

Thick masses of little weeds float about the surface of the water, and by forming a soft pulp, contribute an effectual aid to bind together the masses of vegetation. Like a cement, this conglomerate of weeds fills up all the clefts and chasms between the grass and ambatch islands, which are formed in the back-water where the position is sheltered from the winds and free from the influence of the current.

There are two plants, at a superficial glance hardly distinguishable, which perform the largest share in the formation of this compact web. One of them is the thin-membraned water-fern, the *Azolla;* the other (which is quite familiar to every visitor to the tank of the *Victoria regia*) being the *Pistia,* which can hardly fail to recall a head of lettuce. The sailors of the White Nile call it the 'negro tobacco,' probably with reference to the dwarfed growth of the two kinds of tobacco in the negro lands. Besides these, our duck-weeds (*Lemna*) and *Tussiena* of various sorts intertwine themselves with the mass, and the different African representations of our commonest water-plants play a part by no means unimportant.

It is remarkable that in Egypt nearly all the species of water-plants which abound in the stream of the White Nile are wanting entirely ; whilst, on the other hand, all the shore-shrubs, which had their native home in the neighbourhood of the Equator, pass over the intervening districts and there find a settlement. Even the conspicuous ambatch is, in Egypt, not known by name ; and it is quite an event when any of the fragments of the papyrus find their way so far north. Every bit of wood which the river carries in its flood is collected by

the inhabitants of the Nubian Valley, and not a scrap
escapes the keen look-out of the people, who are eager to
compensate for their lack of firewood. At the season
when the waters are at their height, the chase after
floating wood is a daily occupation and a favourite
engagement of the boys.

On February 8 began our actual conflict with this
world of weeds. That entire day was spent in trying
to force our boats along the temporary openings. The
pilots were soon absolutely at a loss to determine by
which channel they ought to proceed. On this account
two vessels were detached from the flotilla to investigate
the possibility of making a passage in a more northerly
direction. Two hundred of our people, sailors and
soldiers, were obliged to tug with ropes for hours together to pull through one boat after the other, while they
walked along the edge of the floating mass, which would
bear whole herds of oxen, as I subsequently had an
opportunity of seeing.

Very singular was the spectacle of the vessels, as
though they had grown in the place where they were,
in the midst of this jungle of papyrus 15 feet high;
whilst the bronzed, swarthy skins of the naked Nubians
contrasted admirably with the bright green which was
everywhere around. The shrieks and shouts with which
they sought to cheer on their work could be heard miles
away. The very hippopotamuses did not seem to like
it ; in their alarm they lifted their heads from the shallows
in which they had stationed themselves for respiration,
and snorted till the gurgling around was horrible. The
sailors, concerned lest by their bulk these unwieldy
creatures should injure the boats — not an unknown
occurrence—gave vent to the full force of their lungs.
This unearthly clamour was indeed the solitary means

of defence at their command; in such a turmoil—men
and boats in every direction—firing a shot was not to be
thought of.

*   *   *   *   *

Up with the sun, with sails hoisted with a moderate
breeze in our favour, off we were on the following morning; short-lived, however, was our propitious start.
Too soon the open water branched out into a labyrinth
of channels, and the bewildered navigators lost all clue
as to the actual direction of the stream.   The projections
of the green islets were always crowned with huge
clumps of papyrus, which here grows in detached
masses.   It probably delights most in quiet waters,
and so does not attain to the form of a high, unbroken
hedge, as on the upper banks of the Gazelle, for here,
on account of the numerous stoppages, the stream flows
through the narrow channels with extraordinary violence.
The strength of the stream often makes towing impractic-
able, and the sailors often have considerable difficulty in
sailing through it to the papyrus bushes when they want
to attach to their solid stems the ropes which are thrown
out from their boats.   This was the way in which we
from sheer necessity sustained the resistance of the
current.   The depth of the channel was quite sufficient
in itself to allow us to proceed, as our vessels drew only
three feet of water; but the passage had become so
contracted that at sunset we fastened ourselves to the
papyrus-stems, quite despairing of ever being able to
make further progress in this direction.

It was one of those marvellous nights when the unwonted associations of a foreign clime seem to leave an
indelible impression on the memory of the traveller.
Here were the dazzling sparks of the glow-worm glaring
upon us like a greeting from our far-off home, and in

countless masses glittering upon the dewy stalks of the
floating prairie. In the midst of these were fastened our
boats, hemmed in as firmly as though they were enclosed
by Polar ice. Loud was the rushing of the stream as it
forced a way along its contracted course; but louder
still was the incessant splashing of the emerging hippopotamuses, which had been driven by the vessels, as it
were, into a corner, and were at a loss, like ourselves,
how to go on or to retreat. Until daybreak their dis-
quietude continued, and it seemed as though their
numbers kept increasing till there was quite a crowd
of them.

Already during the afternoon they had afforded a
singular sight. Whilst about half of our men were
wading in shallow water, and straining at the ropes,
they found that they had entirely enclosed no less than
six hippopotamuses, whose huge flesh-coloured carcases,
dappled with brown, rose above the surface of the water
in a way but rarely seen. A cross-fire was opened upon
them from several vessels, but I could not make any use
of my elephant-rifle, because about 200 of our men were
towing upon my line of sight. The clumsy brutes
snorted and bellowed, and rolled against each other in
their endeavours to escape; their ponderous weight bore
down the tangle of the water-growth, and the splashing
was prodigious.

Four days had now been consumed in this strain and
struggle; after a final and unavailing effort on the fifth
day, there seemed no alternative but to go back, and
make trial of another and more northerly branch of this
bewildering canal-system. We succeeded in our retro-
grade movement so far as to attain an open basin, and
found that we had only the distance of about 200 feet to
get over in order that we might reach the spot whereat

the various streams of the Upper Nile unite. This place on the maps is distinguished by the name of Lake No, but the sailors always call it Mogren-el-Bohoor, *i.e.*, the mouth of the streams. The difficulties which met us here were apparently quite hopeless. Our boats were not only heavily laden with corn, but, formed of the heaviest wood, their build was unusually broad and massive. Yet, heavy and unwieldy as they were, there was no alternative than literally to drag them over the grass. By dint, however, of main force, before the day was out the task was accomplished. The grass mass itself was lifted and pushed in front, whilst the men turned their backs against the sides of the boats, and pressed them on from behind. I was the only passenger to remain on board, because, being fearful of a chill, which might result in fever, I could not venture into the water.

12. THE VICTORIA NYANZA REACHED.

CAPTAIN SPEKE, 1858.*

Many may remember the excitement produced by an ordinary map, and a more extraordinary lake figuring upon it, of a rather slug-like shape, which drew forth risible observations from all who entered the Royal Geographical Society's rooms in the year 1856. In order to ascertain the truthfulness of the said map, the Royal Geographical Society appointed Captain Burton to investigate this monster piece of water, represented as lying at a distance of 700 miles inland west from Zanzibar.

As Captain Burton and myself had been engaged on a former occasion exploring the Somali country in

* 'Speke's Journal,' *Blackwood's Magazine*, vol. lxxxvi.

Eastern Africa together, he invited me to join in these investigations.

*   *   *   *   *

The Church missionaries, residing for many years at Zanzibar, are the prime and first promoters of this discovery.

*   *   *   *   *

Amongst the more important disclosures made by the Arabs was a constant reference to a large lake or inland sea, which their caravans were in the habit of visiting. It was a singular thing that, at whatever part of the coast the missionaries arrived, on inquiring from the travelling merchants where they went to, they one and all stated to an inland sea, the dimensions of which were such that nobody could give any estimate of its length or width. Their accounts seemed to indicate a single sheet of water.

*   *   *   *   *

Our line of march, about 600 rectilinear geographical miles, had been nearly due west from Zanzibar. . . . We began to ascend at the eastern horn of a large crescent-shaped mass of mountains overhanging the northern half of the Tanganyika Lake, which I am now about to describe to you. This mountain mass I consider to be THE TRUE MOUNTAINS OF THE MOON, regarding which so many erroneous speculations have been ventured. I infer this because they lie beyond Unyamuézi (country of the moon), and must have been first mentioned to geographical inquirers by the Wan-yamuézi (people of the moon), who have from time out of mind visited the coast, and must have been the first who gave information of them. I am the more satisfied of the correctness of this view from remembering the common Greek practice of changing significant general names into equivalents in their own tongue, and the consequent probability of their calling these mountains after the men who live near them.

*   *   *   *   *

As in its present state your atlas presents a blank instead of one of the most beautiful inland seas in the world, you would be glad, perhaps, to know its position and dimensions, which will enable you to lay it down on the map yourself. The Tanganyika Lake, lying between 3° and 8° south latitude, and in 29° east longitude, has a length of 300 miles, and is from thirty to forty broad in its centre, but tapers towards each end. The surface-level, as I ascertained by the temperature of boiling water, is only 1,800 feet, and it appears quite sunk into the lap of these mountains.

*   *   *   *   *

I then proposed that . . . we should travel northwards in search of a lake, said by the Arabs to be both broader and longer than the Tanganyika, and which they call Ukerewé, after the island where their caravans go for ivory. This lake has no significant name. The negroes, in speaking of it, merely say Nyanza (or the Lake). My companion was, most unfortunately, quite done up, but very graciously consented to wait with the Arabs and recruit his health, whilst I should proceed alone and satisfy the Royal Geographical Society's desires as far as possible about all the inland seas, the object for which they sent us, and which it was, therefore, our utmost desire to accomplish.

*   *   *   *   *

And now I am ready to lead you over my second voyage of discovery—the one which, to my mind, is by far the most satisfactory, and I trust it will be so to you, for it takes you into the richest part of Africa, and discloses to you the probable and, I believe, true source of that mighty stream the Nile; and has almost, if not entirely, solved a problem which it has been the first geographical desideratum of many thousand years to ascertain, and the ambition of the first monarchs of the world to unravel. . . .

The caravan, after quitting Isamiro, began winding up a long but gradually inclined hill—which, as it bears no native name, I will call Somerset—until it reached its summit, when the vast expanse of the pale-blue waters of the Nyanza burst suddenly upon my gaze. It was early morning. The distant sea-line of the north horizon was defined in the calm atmosphere between the north and west points of the compass; but even this did not afford me any idea of the breadth of the lake, as an archipelago of islands . . . rising to a height of 200 or 300 feet above the water, intersected the line of vision to the left; while on the right the western horn of the Ukerewé Island cut off any further view of its distant waters to the eastward of north. A sheet of water—an elbow of the sea, however, at the base of the low range on which I stood—extended far away to the eastward, to where, in the dim distance, a hummock-like elevation of the mainland marked what I understood to be the south and east angle of the lake. . . .

This view was one which, even in a well-known and explored country, would have arrested the traveller by its peaceful beauty. The islands, each swelling in a gentle slope to a rounded summit, clothed with wood between the rugged, angular, closely-cropping rocks of granite, seemed mirrored in the calm surface of the lake, on which I here and there detected a small black speck, the tiny canoe of some Muanza fisherman. On the gently shelving plain below me, blue smoke curled above the trees, which here and there partially concealed villages and hamlets, their brown thatched roofs contrasting with the emerald green of the beautiful milk-bush, the coral branches of which cluster in such profusion round the cottages, and form alleys and hedge-rows about the villages as ornamental as any garden-shrub in England. But the pleasure of the mere view vanished in the presence of those more intense and exciting emotions which are called up by the consideration of the commercial and geographical importance of the prospect before me. I no longer felt any doubt that the lake at my feet gave birth to that interesting river, the source of which has been the subject of so much speculation, and the object of so many explorers. The Arabs' tale was proved to the letter. This is a far more extensive lake than the Tanganyika; 'so broad you could not see across it, and so long that nobody knew its length.'

*   *   *   *   *

13. OUTFALL OF THE NILE FROM THE VICTORIA NYANZA.

CAPTAIN J. H. SPEKE,* 1862.

The 'Stones,' as the Waganda call the falls, was by far the most interesting sight I had seen in Africa. Everybody ran to see them at once, though the march had been long and fatiguing, and even my sketch-block was called into play. Though beautiful, the scene was not exactly what I expected; for the broad surface of the lake was shut out from view by a spur of hill, and the falls, about 12 feet deep, and 400 to 500 feet broad, were broken by rocks. Still, it was a sight that attracted

* ' Discovery of the Source of the Nile.' (Blackwood, 1863.)

THE RIPON FALLS ON THE NILE.

one to it for hours. The roar of the waters, the thousands of passenger-fish leaping at the falls with all their might, the Wasoga and Waganda fishermen coming out in boats and taking posts on all the rocks with rod and hook, hippopotami and crocodiles lying sleepily on the water, the ferry at work above the falls, and cattle driven down to drink at the margin of the lake, made in all, with the pretty nature of the country—small hills, grassy-topped, with trees in the folds, and gardens on the lower slopes— as interesting a picture as one could wish to see.

The expedition had now performed its functions. I saw that old Father Nile without any doubt rises in the Victoria Nyanza, and, as I had foretold, that lake is the great source of the holy river which cradled the first expounder of our religious belief.

* * * * *

The most remote waters, *or top head of the Nile*, is the southern end of the lake, situated close on the third degree of south latitude, which gives to the Nile the surprising length, in direct measurement, rolling over thirty-four degrees of latitude, of above 2,300 miles, or more than one-eleventh of the circumference of our globe.

14. DISCOVERY OF THE ALBERT NYANZA.

SIR SAMUEL BAKER.[*] 1863.

I had been fifteen days waiting at Gondokoro when suddenly I heard guns firing in the south, and my men rushed into my cabin, saying that the trader's party had arrived with two white men—*Englishmen*—in their company, who had come from the sea! It is impossible to describe that moment. Quixotic dreams that I had

* · Proceedings of the Royal Geographical Society,' vol. x.

cherished were now realized, and in a few minutes later I met those gallant explorers, Captains Speke and Grant, marching along the river's bank, arriving in honourable rags, careworn, haggard, but proud of having won.

Speke was my old friend; but I felt that his brave companion Grant was also an old friend, for such a meeting in the centre of Africa vanquishes all time, and the hearty shake of the hand effects more than the cold acquaintance of years. But one disappointment tinged this happy meeting. I had always hoped to have found them somewhere about the Nile source, and to have shared with them the honour of the discovery. I had my expedition in the most perfect order, and I was ready for any place, however distant. Happily, much remained to be completed. Speke informed me that he had heard from the natives that a large lake existed to the west of Unyoro, which he thought might be a second source of the Nile, as the river flowed into it, and almost immediately after its junction issued from it, and continued its course to Gondokoro. He also said that he and Grant crossed the river at Karuma Falls in about 2° 20' N. lat., where they lost the river as it turned suddenly to the west; therefore it was of the highest importance to explore it from that point to the lake, which he called the Luta N'zigé. I immediately determined to undertake this exploration, feeling convinced that the reported lake had an important position in the basin of the Nile. . . .

We arrived at the Nile at Karuma Falls at the very spot where Speke and Grant had crossed the river, in lat. 2° 17' N. Instead of being welcomed by Kamrasi, as I had expected, we were not allowed to cross the river. Crowds of armed men thronged the heights on the opposite bank to resist our landing. At length, after a long day lost in gesticulating and shouting our peaceful

4

intentions, a boat came across the river with some head-
men of the country, who, after strict examination, pronounced me to be Speke's own brother, ' from one father
and one mother.'

* * * * *

The King did not appear for three days, during which
we were by his orders confined on a wretched marsh on
the south side of the Kafoor River, precisely where Speke
and Grant were located formerly. In rather a suspicious
manner Kamrasi arrived, accompanied by about a thousand
men. I was very ill with fever, and was carried on a litter
to his hut. He was a fine, dignified-looking fellow, well
dressed in bark-cloth, gracefully draped around him, and
beautifully clean in his person ; the nails of his hands
and feet being perfectly white, and carefully attended
to. He gave me seventeen cows, and a quantity of
plantain wine ; accordingly, I presented him with a
variety of objects of value, including a handsome Persian
carpet of most gorgeous colours, which captivated him
immensely. I told him that Speke and Grant had arrived
safely, and had spoken well of him ; therefore I had come
to thank him in the name of my country, and to present
him with a few curiosities. I also told him that the
Queen of my country had taken a great interest in the
discovery of the Nile source, now proved to be within
his dominions, and that I wished to visit the Luta N'zigé
Lake, and descend to the junction and the exit of the
river. He told me that Speke was evidently my brother,
having a beard precisely similar ; that I was far too ill to
attempt the march to the lake—which was the *M'wootan*,
not *Luta N'zigé*—as it was *six months' journey ;* that he
was afraid I might die in his country, and perhaps my
Queen would imagine I had been murdered, and might
accordingly invade his territory. I replied that this was

a perfectly correct idea—that no Englishman could be
murdered with impunity; but that I had resolved not to
leave his country until I had seen the lake, therefore the
sooner the exploration was completed, the less chance
there would be of my dying in his country.

I returned to my hut disheartened. I had now been
fourteen months from Khartúm, struggling against every
species of difficulty; for twelve months I had been
employed in repairing guns, doctoring the sick, and
attending the wounded of the ivory hunter's party,
simply to gain sufficient influence to enable me to procure porters. That accomplished, I had arrived at this
spot, M'rooli, in lat. 1° 37′ N., only six days' march from
the Victoria Lake; and I had hoped that a ten days'
westerly march would enable me to reach the M'wootan
N'zigé. I now heard that it was *six months' journey !* I
was ill with daily fever, my wife likewise. I had no
quinine, neither any supplies, such as coffee, tea, etc.;
nothing but water and the common food of the natives—
good enough when in strong health, but uneatable in
sickness.

That night passed heavily ; the following morning, to
my dismay, every one of my porters had deserted. They
had heard the King declare the journey to the lake to be
six months, and all had absconded. Day after day I had
interviews with the King Kamrasi, whose only object
in seeing me was to extort all I had. I gave him everything he asked for except my sword : this was what he
coveted.

The traders obtained a large quantity of ivory and
left the country, leaving me, with my thirteen men, sick
and hopeless. I would not be persuaded to return ; I
felt sure that the lake was not so far distant. Hearing that
the trade from the lake consisted of salt, I found a native

dealer, and from him I obtained the cheering information that the lake was only fifteen days distant. The King had deceived me, merely wishing to detain me with him in order to strip me of everything. At length I gave him the coveted sword and a double-barrelled gun ; my head-man drank blood with him as a proof of amity, and he gave me two chiefs as guides and about three hundred men as escort. These fellows were dressed like our juvenile ideas of devils, having horns upon their heads, and were grotesquely got up with false beards made of the bushy ends of cows' tails. This motley escort gave much trouble on the journey, plundering the villages *en route*, and drawing all supplies before we had a chance of procuring anything. I therefore discharged my attendants after a few days' march, and continued the journey with my guides and porters. Every day the porters, apparently without reason, would suddenly throw their loads down and bolt into the high grass, disappearing like so many rabbits. This occasioned much delay, as fresh men had to be collected from distant villages.

Marching for some days along the south bank of the Kafoor River, we had to cross this deep stream at a muddy ford ; in crossing this river my wife suddenly fell, apparently dead, struck by a *coup de soleil*. For seven days she was carried in a state of insensibility along our melancholy route ; the rain in torrents, the country a series of swamps and forest and grass jungle ; no possibility of resting in one place, as there was nothing to eat on the road, and our provisions were insufficient. The people put a new handle to the pickaxe to dig her grave, and looked for a dry spot. I was utterly exhausted with fever and watching, and, after a long march, I fell senseless by the side of her litter. The next morning a miraculous change had taken place, which I can never forget.

After eighteen days' journey through a park-like country from M'rooli, the long-wished-for lake was announced by the guide. For three days I had seen a high range of mountains, apparently about eighty miles distant, and I had feared that these lay between me and the lake; to my great joy I now heard that they formed the opposite or western shore. Suddenly, upon reaching some rising ground, the great reservoir of the Nile lay before me! Far below, some 1,500 feet beneath a precipitous cliff of granite, lay my prize so hardly sought— a boundless sea-horizon south and south-west; while west, the faint blue mountains, of about 7,000 feet above the water-level, hemmed in the glorious expanse of waters.

Weak and exhausted with more than twelve months' anxiety, toil, and sickness, I tottered down the steep and zigzag path, and in about two hours I reached the shore. The waves were rolling upon a beach of sand; and as I drank the water and bathed my face in the welcome flood with a feeling of true gratitude for success, I named this great basin of the Nile (subject to Her Majesty's permission) the 'Albert Nyanza,' in memory of a great man who had passed away. The Victoria and the Albert Lakes are the reservoirs of the Nile.

15. THE BAHR-AL-GHAZAL.

DR. G. SCHWEINFURTH.*

One of the objects contemplated in my journey was to show the importance of the western affluents of the Nile which unite in the Gazelle; and I have given evidence that, one way and another, they traverse a region

* 'The Heart of Africa.' (S. Low and Co., 1878.)

of not less than 150,000 square miles. When I mention
that in 1863 Speke called the Gazelle ‘an unimportant
branch,’* and, moreover, that Baker has spoken of its
magnitude with great depreciation, in reply I might
allude to another interesting fact in geographical annals.
Not only did Bruce, a hundred years ago, suppose that
he had discovered the sources of the Nile in Abyssinia,
just where a hundred years previously they had been
marked upon the Portuguese maps; but he represented
the Bahr-el-Abiad as an inconsiderable stream, which
joined the stream of his discovery at Halfaya, Khartoom
at that time being not in existence. But it is absolutely
impossible that Bruce could have returned from Sennaar
to Berber along the left bank of the Blue Nile, and could
have crossed at its mouth from the very spot where
Khartoom now stands, without being aware that close
behind him there was rolling its waters a stream as broad
again as the Blue Nile. The record of his travels does
not contain one word about the White Nile. The plain
truth is that the White Nile was overlooked and dis-
paraged, because it would have thrown his Blue Nile in
the shade.†

    *   *   *   *   *

The volume of water brought by the Gazelle to swell
the Nile is still an unsolved problem. In the contention
as to which stream is entitled to rank as first-born among
the children of the great river-god, the Bahr-el-Ghazal
has apparently a claim in every way as valid as the Bahr-

* Speke, p. 609: ‘We found only a small piece of water, resembling a duck-pond, buried in a sea of rushes.’

† The words of the far-famed traveller are: ‘It runs from Sennaar
past many considerable villages, which are inhabited by white men
of Arabia. Here it passes by Gerri [now Khartoom], in a north-
easterly direction, so as to join the Tacazze’ (Bruce, bk. vi., c. 14).

el-Gebel. In truth, it would appear to stand in the same relation to the Bahr-el-Gebel as the White Nile does to the Blue. At the season when the waters are highest, the inundations of the Gazelle spread over a very wide territory ; about March, the time of year when they are lowest, the river settles down, in its upper section, into a number of vast pools of nearly stagnant water, whilst its lower portion runs off into divers narrow and sluggish channels. These channels, overgrown as they look with massy vegetation, conceal beneath (either in their open depth or mingled with the unfathomable abyss of mud) such volumes of water as defy our reckoning.

The Gazelle then it is which gives to the White Nile a sufficient impetus to roll its waters onward ; subsequently the Bahr-el-Gebel finds its way and contributes a more powerful element to the progress of the stream. It must all along be borne in mind that there are besides two other streams, the Dyoor and the Bahr-el-Arab, each of them more important than any tributary of the Bahr-el-Gebel, and these bring in their own influence. To estimate aright the true relation of all these various tributaries is ever opening up the old question in a new light.

16. RUWENZORI.

Sir H. M. STANLEY,* 1888.

'Round this gulf live Ethiopians, who are cannibals, and westward of them stretches the Mountain of the Moon, the snows from which are received by the lakes of the Nile.'—PTOLEMY, 'Geography' (A.D. 150), iv. 8, 3.

When about five miles from Nsabé camp, while looking to the south-east, and meditating upon the events of the

* 'In Darkest Africa.' (S. Low and Co., 1890.)

last month, my eyes were directed by a boy to a mountain said to be covered with salt, and I saw a peculiar-shaped cloud of a most beautiful silver colour, which assumed the proportions and appearance of a vast mountain covered with snow. Following its form downward, I became struck with the deep blue-black colour of its base, and wondered if it portended another tornado; then as the sight descended to the gap between the eastern and western plateaus, I became for the first time conscious that what I gazed upon was not the image or semblance of a vast mountain, but the solid substance of a real one, with its summit covered with snow. I ordered a halt, and examined it carefully with a field-glass, then took a compass bearing of the centre of it, and found it bear 215° magnetic. It now dawned upon me that this must be the Ruwenzori, which was said to be covered with a white metal or substance believed to be rock, as reported by Kavalli's two slaves.

*   *   *   *   *

On that day it was visible for hours. On surmounting the table-land, the next day or so, it had disappeared.

On returning for the third time to the Nyanza, in January, 1889, and during our long stay at Kavalli for two and a half months, it was unseen, until suddenly casting our eyes, as usual, towards that point where it ought to be visible, the entire length of the range burst out of the cloudy darkness, and gratified over a thousand pairs of anxious eyes that fixed their gaze upon the singular and magnificent scene.

*   *   *   *   *

It will then be understood that a transparent atmosphere is very rare in this region, and that had our stay been as short as that of previous travellers, Ruwenzori might have remained longer unknown.

    *   *   *   *   *

In one of the darkest corners of the earth, shrouded by perpetual mist, brooding under the eternal storm-clouds, surrounded by darkness and mystery, there has been hidden to this day a giant among mountains, the melting snow of whose tops has been for some fifty centuries most vital to the peoples of Egypt. Imagine to what a God the reverently-inclined primal nations would have exalted this mountain, which from such a far-away region as this contributed so copiously to their beneficent and sacred Nile. And this thought of the beneficent Nile brings on another. In fancy we look down along that crooked silver vein to where it disports and spreads out to infuse new life to Egypt near the Pyramids, some 4,000 miles away, where we beheld populous swarms of men—Arabs, Copts, Fellahs, Negroes, Turks, Greeks, Italians, Frenchmen, English, Germans, and Americans —bustling, jostling, or lounging; and we feel a pardonable pride in being able to inform them for the first time that much of the sweet water they drink, and whose virtues they so often exalt, issues from the deep and extensive snow-beds of Ruwenzori or Ruwenjura—' the Cloud-King.'

    *   *   *   *   *   •

We claim to have located with reasonable precision the grand old Mountains of the Moon.

PART II.

THE GREAT DESERTS AND BORDERING REGIONS.

INTRODUCTION.

THE great desert which, cleft near its eastern edge by the valley of the Nile, extends over Northern Africa from the Atlantic to the Red Sea, is, of course, a principal reason why the rest of the continent has so long been a land of mystery and seclusion, with men and animals unlike those of other parts of the world. But it is itself among the most interesting regions upon that continent, and numberless travellers have acknowledged its fascination, even though it may have taught them to think water the most precious thing on earth, and to regard the sun as an enemy, like the people of old (see 20), whose creed seems so strange to the European. Part of its charm is, no doubt, that it is a region in which time makes no alteration in the aspect of the country, and little in the manners of men. The oasis of Augila, now generally written Aujileh, where the Nasamonians gathered dates, has still its date-palms, and its ancient name; and the merchants journeying through it measure their distances still as so many days' journey from one habitable spot to another. For the desert has its patches of fertile land, some large and some small, where trees grow and water may be found, compared in ancient times to the isolated

spots on the yellow hide of a panther. The name of
' oasis ' which we give to these spots is of old Egyptian
origin, and is used by Herodotus (see 18), who, however,
knew it only as the name of one particular region, that
which is marked on modern maps as the Greater Oasis,
due west from the ruins of Luxor and Karnak, which are
the remains of the Egyptian Thebes. The Temple of
Ammon, which the Persian conqueror Cambyses desired
to burn, was in what is now called the oasis of Siwah, a
place at the present day scarcely ever seen by Europeans,
but renowned of old for its temple, of which only a few
ruins are left, and for the visit paid to it by a mightier
conqueror than Cambyses, Alexander the Great. Cambyses himself is supposed to have made his disastrous
march through the desert of Korosko, well known in the
story of our latest Egyptian campaign.

Since Islam invaded the African deserts—and at present practically all the inhabitants of the Sahara, whether
Arabs or, like the Tuaregs, of Berber origin, are Mohammedans at least in name—the dangers which the European
traveller in that region must always have undergone from
the wilderness, and from the tendency of nomadic peoples
to adopt the habits of robbers, have been greatly increased
by religious antipathy. For this reason most of these
travellers have attempted to disguise their faith and
nationality, and have run great risks in case of detection.
Of all the hidden places of the desert to which such
adventurous spirits have longed to penetrate none, not
excepting the vaguely-reported Lake Tchad, which
might, it was thought, turn out to contain the secret of
the Niger (see 38), was more attractive than the famous
city of Timbuctoo, lying on the northern bank of that
mysterious river. Several centuries ago it was a place
of great name and importance, which, however, had been

considerably diminished before Barth (26) succeeded in
entering it.　Within the last twenty years the French
have been able to reach Timbuctoo by the Niger ; but
the Niger itself was to former generations inaccessible,
and all the earlier attempts to reach the city were made
by way of the desert.　Only one European that entered
Timbuctoo during the nineteenth century before Barth
returned home to tell the tale of his achievement.

17. A DESCRIPTION OF THE DESERT.

CAPTAIN G. F. LYON,* 1818.

In no part of the Desert which I have seen, or of which
I could obtain accounts, does it appear that water is
found on the surface ; hence it seems extraordinary that
wild animals should exist, yet antelopes, buffaloes, and
some other animals are, in different places, very
numerous.　Rats are frequently found to burrow in
plains twenty or thirty miles distant from shrubs, and
their food is unknown, no birds being found there, and
the small lizards and snakes, as well as the few insects,
being too active to be caught by them.　In some parts,
the only living creature seen for many days is a small
insect, somewhat resembling a spider, called Naga
t'Allah, or the ' She-camel of God.'　Beetles are also
seen where kafflés rest, or in the vicinity of shrubs, and
their curious tracks in the sand are so marked that I
have sometimes traced the same insect for a mile or two
as I rode along.

Nothing can be more awful than the stillness which
prevails, more particularly when the surface is sandy.　I
have sometimes walked at night from the kafflé so as to

* ' Travels in Northern Africa.'　(Murray, 1821.)

be beyond the noise made by the camels or horses, and have experienced a sensation I am unable to describe, as I felt the wind blow past me, and heard the sound which my figure caused it to make by arresting its progress. Near towns, or in places where animals can exist, the slow melancholy cry of the hyæna or jackal is frequently heard during the night when these animals prowl round the kafflé.

The appearance of water on the sandy and gravelly deserts is very frequent, and is generally so well defined that it would be difficult to distinguish it from a river, were it possible that both could be seen at the same time. It is called Shrab by the Arabs, who often amused themselves by calling to us that water was in sight, until we became accustomed to the appearance. Of this curious phenomenon so much has been said by various writers that any attempt at description on my part would be unnecessary. The looming of objects when the sun is at its greatest strength is very striking, as from the vapour which rises they are, at a slight distance, much obscured. I have frequently, in riding along, been delighted at observing in the distance a tree which appeared sufficiently large to shade me from the sun, and to allow of my reposing under it until the camels came up, and have often quickened my pace in consequence, until, on a near approach, it has proved to be nothing more than a bush which did not throw a shade sufficient even to shelter one of my hands. Sand-hills deceive still more, always appearing very distant when the sun is on them, and it has often happened that I have been startled by seeing a man or camel rise close to me on the top of one of the apparently distant hills. The excessive dryness of the Desert is in some places very extraordinary, particularly to the southward of the

Soudah Mountains, where, in going to as well as coming from Fezzan, I observed that our clothes, and the tails of our horses, emitted electric sparks.

18. THE ATTEMPT OF CAMBYSES TO CROSS THE DESERT.*

B.C. 525.

When the spies had seen everything, they departed on their return journey. And Cambyses, when he heard their story, fell into a great rage, and marched at once against the Ethiopians. He gave no orders for the collection of supplies, nor troubled himself to consider that he was starting to march to the ends of the earth ; but, like an unreasoning madman, must set off as soon as he heard from his messengers, ordering the Greeks whom he had with him to remain where they were, but taking all his infantry with him. When his expedition arrived at Thebes, he detached a force of some fifty thousand, with orders to make slaves of the people of Ammon, and burn the oracle of Zeus ; while he himself, with the rest of the army, proceeded against the Ethiopians. But before his force had made good the fifth part of the journey, all that they had in the way of supplies had given out, and after the supplies the beasts of burden were eaten, and gave out too.

Now, if Cambyses, when he found this out, had repented himself, and led his army back again, he might have finished like a wise man what was begun in folly ; but instead of this, he took no account of it, and marched onward as before. Now, the soldiers, so long as they could find anything growing, kept themselves alive by

* ' Herodotus,' iii. 25, 26.

eating herbs ; but when they came to the sand, certain of them did a terrible thing, for they cast lots among every ten of them, and ate the man on whom the lot fell. When Cambyses heard of the cannibalism he was alarmed, and giving up the expedition against the Ethiopians, returned and came to Thebes, with the loss of great numbers of his men ; and from Thebes he went down the river to Memphis, and sent the Greeks back by sea.

This was the end of the Ethiopian expedition. But as for those who were sent to march against the Ammonians, it is certainly known that, after starting from Thebes under the direction of guides, they came to the city Oasis, which is held by Samians, said to belong to the Aeschrionian tribe ; they are seven days' journey through the desert from Thebes, and the place is called, in the Greek language, 'the Island of the Blest.' So far as this place the story of their march is known, but as to what happened afterwards no one, unless it be the Ammonians themselves and those who heard it from them, has anything to say about them, for they neither got through to the Ammonians nor returned back again. However, the story told about them by the Ammonians themselves is this, that they were marching from this Oasis through the desert to attack them, and had reached a spot about half-way between them and Oasis when, as they were taking their noonday meal, there rose up a great and terrible wind from the south, which brought the sand upon them in heaps and buried them, and so they vanished out of sight. Such, say the Ammonians, was the fate of this expedition.

19. SANDSTORMS.

J. BRUCE,[*] 1770.

We were here at once surprised and terrified by a sight surely one of the most magnificent in the world. In tha vast expanse of desert, from W. and to N.W. of us, we saw a number of prodigious pillars of sand at different distances, at times moving with great celerity, at others stalking on with a majestic slowness; at intervals we thought they were coming in a very few minutes to overwhelm us; and small quantities of sand did actually more than once reach us. Again they would retreat so as to be almost out of sight, their tops reaching to the very clouds. There the tops often separated from the bodies; and these, once disjoined, dispersed in the air, and did not appear more.

Sometimes they were broken near the middle, as if struck with a large cannon shot. About noon they began to advance with considerable swiftness upon us, the wind being very strong at north. Eleven of them ranged alongside of us about the distance of three miles. The greatest diameter of the largest appeared to me at that distance as if it would measure ten feet. They retired from us with a wind at S.E., leaving an impression upon my mind to which I can give no name, though surely one ingredient in it was fear, with a considerable deal of wonder and astonishment. It was in vain to think of flying; the swiftest horse, or fastest sailing ship, could be of no use to carry us out of this danger, and the full persuasion of this riveted me as if to the spot where I stood. . . .

The whole of our company were much disheartened

[*] 'Travels to Discover the Source of the Nile.'

(except Idris), and imagined that they were advancing into whirlwinds of moving sand, from which they should never be able to extricate themselves; but before four o'clock in the afternoon these phantoms of the plain had all of them fallen to the ground and disappeared. In the evening we came to Waadi Dimokea, where we passed the night, much disheartened, and our fear more increased, when we found, upon wakening in the morning, that one side was perfectly buried in the sand that the wind had blown above us in the night.

From this day, subordination, though not entirely ceased, was fast on the decline ; all was discontent, murmuring, and fear. Our water was greatly diminished, and that terrible death by thirst began to stare us in the face. . . .

The same appearance of moving pillars of sand presented themselves to us this day in form and disposition like those we had seen at Waadi Halboub, only they seemed to be more in number, and less in size. They came several times in a direction close upon us; that is, I believe, within less than two miles. They began, immediately after sun-rise, like a thick wood, and almost darkened the sun : his rays shining through them for near an hour, gave them an appearance of pillars of fire. Our people now became desperate : the Greeks shrieked out, and said it was the day of judgment. Ismael pronounced it to be hell, and the Tucorories, that the world was on fire. I asked Idris if ever he had before seen such a sight. He said he had often seen them as terrible, though never worse ; but what he feared most was that extreme redness in the air, which was a sure presage of the coming of the simoom.

* * * * *

On the 16th . . . at eleven o'clock, while we contemplated with great pleasure the rugged top of Chiggre, to which we were fast approaching, and where we were to solace ourselves with plenty of good water, Idris cried out, with a loud voice, ' Fall upon your faces, for here is the simoom.' I saw from the S.E. a haze come, in colour like the purple part of the rainbow, but not so compressed or thick. It did not occupy twenty yards in breadth, and was about twelve feet high from the ground. It was a kind of blush upon the air, and it moved very rapidly, for I scarce could turn to fall upon the ground with my head to the northward, when I felt the heat of its current plainly upon my face. We all lay flat on the ground, as if dead, till Idris told us it was blown over. The meteor, or purple haze, which I saw, was indeed passed, but the light air that still blew was of heat to threaten suffocation. For my part, I found distinctly in my breast that I had imbibed a part of it, nor was I free of an asthmatic sensation till I had been some months in Italy, at the baths of Poretta, near two years afterwards.

20. THE DWELLERS IN THE DESERT 2,000 YEARS AGO.*

Further to the west dwell the Nasamonians, a numerous people, who in summer leave their flocks upon the sea-shore, and go up to the region of Augila to gather the fruit of the date-palms, many of which grow there, and great trees too, all bearing fruit. They catch locusts, too, and after drying them in the sun, pound them small, and then sprinkling them upon their milk, drink them up. . . .

And ten days' journey from Augila is a hill of salt, and a spring of fresh water, and many date-bearing

* Herodotus, iv. 172, 183, 184.

palm-trees. And here too are men dwelling, called the Garamantes, a very large nation, who sow their crops by putting earth upon the top of the salt. In their land we find the oxen that feed backwards, and this is the reason they feed backwards: they have their horns curving forwards, and therefore go backwards as they graze, for they cannot go forwards because their horns keep striking into the ground. They differ in nowise from other oxen, save in this one matter, and in the thickness and hardness of their hides. These Garamantes hunt the cave-dwelling Ethiopians in chariots drawn by four horses, for the cave-dwelling Ethiopians are swiftest-footed of all men whose history has come to our knowledge. The cave-dwellers eat snakes and lizards, and other such creeping things; and they have a speech like no other on earth, but squeak in the manner of bats.

And yet ten days' further journey from the Garamantes is another hill of salt, and a spring, and men dwelling thereby called the Atarantes, who alone of all men within our knowledge have no names. The name of Atarantes they indeed have in common, but no one man of them has a name to himself. These people curse the sun as he rises to his height, and reproach him with insults of every kind, because he afflicts them with burning heat, themselves the inhabitants and the land they inhabit. And again, ten days' further journey, another hill of salt, and a spring, and men dwelling thereby. And hard by this salt-hill is a mountain named Atlas; it is narrow and rounded on all sides, and it is said to be so high that the tops of it cannot be seen, since the clouds never depart from them, neither in summer nor yet in winter. And the natives of the country say that it is the pillar which supports the

heavens. These natives have their name from their
mountain, for they are called Atlantes. And it is said
that they eat nothing that has life, and that they never
have dreams.

21. THE SAME REGION A CENTURY AGO.

F. HORNEMAN,* 1797.

The Tibbo are not quite black, their growth is slender,
their limbs are well turned, their walk is light and swift,
their eyes are quick, their lips thick, their nose is not
turned up, and not large, their hair is very long, but less
curled than that of the Negroes. They appear to have
much natural capacity, but they have too few oppor-
tunities of improving it, being surrounded by barbarous
nations, or Mahometans. Their intercourse with the
Arabs, to whom they convey slaves, has probably corrupted them ; they are accused of being mistrustful,
treacherous, and deceitful. The Fezzanians do not
travel singly with them, for they are afraid of being
surprised and murdered at the instigation of the company with whom they travel. The language of the
Tibbo is spoken with extraordinary rapidity, and has
many consonants, particularly the L and S.

*   *   *   *   .   *

It is singular that the people of Augila, in speaking of
these tribes, make much the same comparison which
Herodotus ('Melpom.,' c. 183) does when speaking of the
Ethiopian *Troglodytæ*, hunted by the Garamantes, ' that
their language is like the whistling of birds.'

* ' Travels from Cairo to Mourzouk.' (London, 1802.)

22. THE NOMAD ARABS.

MAJOR DENHAM,* 1822.

Arabs are generally thin, meagre figures, though possessing expressive and sometimes handsome features, great violence of gesture and muscular action. Irritable and fiery, they are unlike the dwellers in towns and cities; noisy and loud, their common conversational intercourse appears to be a continual strife and quarrel; they are, however, brave, eloquent, and deeply sensible of shame. I have known an Arab of the lower class refuse his food for days together, because in a skirmish his gun had missed fire; to use his own words, ' Gulbi wahr' (' My heart aches '); ' bindikti kedip hashimtni gedam el naz ' (' my gun lied, and shamed me before the people '). Much has been said of their want of cleanliness; I should, however, without hesitation, pronounce them to be much more cleanly than the lower order of people in any European country. . . .

The fondness of an Arab for traditional history of the most distinguished actions of their remote ancestors is proverbial. Professed story-tellers are ever the appendages to a man of rank. His friends will assemble before his tent, or on the platforms with which the houses of the Moorish Arabs are roofed, and there listen, night after night, to a continued history for sixty or sometimes one hundred nights together. It is a great exercise of genius, and a peculiar gift, held in high estimation amongst them. They have a quickness and clearness of delivery, with a perfect command of words,. surprising to a European ear; they never hesitate, are never at a loss. Their descriptions are highly poetical, and their

* ' Travels in Northern and Central Africa.' (Murray, 1826.)

relations exemplified by figure and metaphor the most
striking and appropriate. Their extempore songs are
also full of fire, and possess many beautiful and happy
similes. Certain tribes are celebrated for this gift of
extempore speaking and singing ; the chiefs cultivate
the propensity in their children, and it is often possessed
to an astonishing degree by men who are unable either
to read or write.

Arabic songs go to the heart, and excite greatly the
passions. I have seen a circle of Arabs straining their
eyes with a fixed attention at one moment, and bursting
with loud laughter ; at the next melting into tears, and
clasping their hands in all the ecstasy of grief and
sympathy.

Their attachment to pastoral life is ever favourable to
love. Many of these children of the desert possess
intelligence and feeling which belong not to the savage,
accompanied by an heroic courage and a thorough con-
tempt of every mode of gaining their livelihood except
by the sword and gun. An Arab values himself chiefly
on his expertness in arms and horsemanship, and on
hospitality.

     *   *   *   *   *

Arabs have always been commended by the ancients
for the fidelity of their attachments, and they are still
scrupulously exact to their words, and respectful to their
kindred. They have been universally celebrated for
their quickness of apprehension and penetration, and the
vivacity of their wit. Their language is certainly one
of the most ancient in the world, but it has many dialects.
The Arabs, however, have their vices and their defects ;
they are naturally addicted to war, bloodshed, and
cruelty, and so malicious as scarcely ever to forget an
injury.

AN ARAB WARRIOR.

Their frequent robberies committed on traders and travellers have rendered the name of an Arab almost infamous in Europe. Amongst themselves, however, they are most honest, and true to the rites of hospitality; and towards those whom they receive as friends into their camp everything is open, and nothing ever known to be stolen. Enter but once into the tent of an Arab, and by the pressure of his hand he insures you protection at the hazard of his life. An Arab is ever true to his bread and salt; once eat with him, and a knot of friendship is tied which cannot easily be loosened.

23. THE TUAREGS.

CAPTAIN G. F. LYON,[*] 1818.

They are the finest race of men I ever saw, tall, straight, and handsome, with a certain air of independence and pride which is very imposing. They are generally white, that is to say, comparatively so; the dark brown of their complexions only being occasioned by the heat of the climate. Their arms or bodies (where constantly covered) are as white as those of many Europeans.

Their costume is very remarkable, and they cover their faces as high as the eyes, in the manner of women on the sea-coast. Their original motive for so doing is now forgotten, but they say it must be right, as it was the fashion of their forefathers. This covering extends as high as half-way up the bridge of the nose, from whence it hangs down below the chin on the breast, much in the same way (but longer) as crape or lace is hung to a lady's half mask. This cloth is generally of blue glazed cotton, but yellow, red, white, and many

* 'Travels in Northern Africa.' (Murray, 1821.)

other colours are worn according to taste, or the ability of the wearer to purchase them. The beard is kept close-clipped, so as not to interfere with the covering, which is tied behind ; their red caps are generally very high, but some wear yellow or green ones, fitted close to the head ; others have no caps at all, but leave their hair to grow, and plait it in long tresses. All wear turbans, which are never of any fixed colour ; blue is the most common and cheap, but gaudy hues are preferred. A large loose shirt (having the sleeves the same size as the body), called Tobe, is the common dress ; it is of cotton, generally blue, or blue and white, and is of their own manufacture, although some wear those of Soudan, which are considered the best that are made.

The merchants generally dress very gaudily while in the towns, wearing kaftans of bright red cloth, or very gay silk and cotton striped, which they procure from the Tripoline traders. A leather kaftan is also much worn, of their own manufacture, as are leather shirts of the skins of antelopes, very neatly sewed, and well prepared. Their trousers are not made so full as those of the Moors, as they would in that case be much encumbered in riding their maherries :* they rather resemble those called Cossack trousers, and are made of cotton stuff, dark blue being the most common. Their sandals are the most elegant part of their dress, being made of black leather, with scarlet thongs to brace them to the feet. The ornamental needlework on the inside of the sole is really admirable. They all wear a whip hanging from a belt passed over the left shoulder by the right side.

Their swords are straight and of great length, and they wield them with much ease and dexterity. From the left wrist is suspended a dagger, with the hilt towards

* Dromedaries.

the hand ; it has a broad leather ring attached to the scabbard, and through this the hand is passed. No Tuarick is ever seen without this appendage, and a light, elegant spear, sometimes entirely of iron, inlaid with brass ; others are of wood, but are also highly ornamented. These weapons are about six feet in length, and are thrown to a great distance. In making war, they have three longer and heavier spears, and a strong lance, which are fastened behind the saddle. A long gun is also generally carried ; and these people are considered sure marksmen.

They are, if possible, more superstitious than the natives of Fezzan, some of them being literally covered with charms against disorders and accidents, which they wear round their arms, legs, necks, across the breast, and, in fact, wherever they can find a place for them. Their spears and guns have also their due allowance, and in the folds of the turbans are always hidden a number of holy writings. Some wear large silver cases tied round the head, containing charms against the devil.

Their language is the Berber, or original African tongue, still spoken in the mountains behind Tunis, in some parts of Morocco, and at Socka, where it is called Ertana. On a future occasion I shall give a small vocabulary of it. They are very proud of the antiquity of their language, which some have told me was spoken by Noah in preference to any other. They never kiss the hand as other Mohammedans do, not even that of the Sultan himself, but advance, and, taking the hand, shake it, and then retire, standing erect, and looking him full in the face—a striking contrast of manners to that of the natives of Fezzan.

No people have more aversion to washing than the Tuarick generally have ; some, after having equipped themselves in a new suit of blue, become so stained for a time as to appear of the same complexion as their garments. Even in performing their necessary purifications, which require that a man should wash in a particular way before his prayers, they avoid water, and make use of sand. Many attempts were made by us to discover the reason why they kept themselves in such a dirty state, but to all our inquiries we obtained nearly the same answers : ' God never intended that man should injure his health if he could avoid it ; water having been given to man to drink, and cook with, it does not agree with the skin of a Tuarick, who always falls sick after much washing.' There are some, however, who do wash, and ridicule the dirty ones, but these are comparatively few.

They are Moslem, and their prayers are in Arabic, of which language many do not understand a syllable ; those who do pray (and there are many who do not) only repeat their belief, viz., ' There is no God but God, and Mohammed is His prophet,' and know very little besides of their religion. They inhabit that immense tract of country known in maps under the name of Sahara, on the Great Desert, and are of numerous tribes, some of whom have no settled habitations, but wander like the Arabs and subsist by plunder. They are not cruel on these occasions, provided they meet with no resistance ; but should the party attacked attempt to defend themselves their death is certain.

24. RUMOURS OF LAKE TCHAD.

CAPTAIN G. F. LYON,* 1818.

Almost every account we received of the Tsād was so materially different, that it long remained a puzzle to us

* ' Travels in Northern Africa.'

how to account for such palpable errors as some of our
informers must have fallen into.   Some declared it to be
so large a lake that the opposite side of it could not be
seen from Birnie; others termed it an inconsiderable
river.   At last, the nephew of the Kadi, who had just
arrived, furnished us with the following clear statement :

'The Tsād is not a river, but an immense lake,
into which many streams discharge themselves after
the summer rains.   It is then for some months of such
extent that the opposite shores cannot be seen, and the
people catch many fish, and go about on it in boats.   In
the early part of the spring, when the great heats come
on, it soon changes its appearance, and dries up, with the
exception of a small rill.   This streamlet, which runs
through the centre of its bed, is called by the same name,
and comes from the westward, taking an easterly direction ; but to what place he knows not.'

25. EXPLORATION OF LAKE TCHAD.

H. BARTH,[*] 1849-1855.

Being tired of the crowd in the town, I mounted on
horseback early next morning in order to refresh myself
with a sight of the lake, which I supposed to be at no
great distance, and indulged beforehand in anticipations
of the delightful view which I fondly imagined was soon
to greet my eye.   We met a good many people and
slaves going out to cut grass for the horses, and leaving
them to their work, we kept on towards the rising sun.   But
no lake was to be seen, and an endless grassy plain without
a single tree extended to the furthest horizon.   At length,
after the grass had increased continually in freshness

* 'Travels in North and Central Africa.   (Longman, 1857.)

and luxuriance, we reached a shallow swamp, the very indented border of which, sometimes bending in, at others bending out, greatly obstructed our progress. Having struggled for a length of time to get rid of this swamp, and straining my eyes in vain to discover the glimmering of an open water in the distance, I at length retraced my steps, consoling myself with the thought that I had seen at least some slight indication of the presence of the watery element, and which seemed indeed to be the only thing which was at present to be seen here.

How different was this appearance of the country from that which it exhibited in the winter from 1854 to 1855, when more than half of the town of Ngórnu was destroyed by the water, and a deep open sea was formed to the south of this place, in which the fertile plain as far as the village of Kúkiya lay buried. This great change seems to have happened in consequence of the lower strata of the ground, which consisted of limestone, having given way in the preceding year, and the whole shore on this side having sunk several feet ; but even without such a remarkable accident, the character of the Tsád is evidently that of an immense lagoon, changing its border every month, and therefore incapable of being mapped with accuracy. Indeed, when I saw to-day the nature of these swampy lowlands surrounding the lake, or rather lagoon, I immediately became aware that it would be quite impossible to survey its shores, even if the state of the countries around should allow us to enter upon such an undertaking. The only thing possible would be on one side to fix the furthest limit reached at times by the inundation of the lagoon, and on the other to determine the extent of the navigable waters.

Having returned to the town, I related to the vizier my unsuccessful excursion in search of the Tsád, and he

obligingly promised to send some horsemen to conduct
me along the shore as far as Káwa, whence I should
return to the capital.

      *   *   *   *   *

With these companions we set out on our excursion,
going north-east, for due east from the town, as I now
learned, the lagoon was at present at more than ten miles'
distance. The fine grassy plain seemed to extend to a
boundless distance, uninterrupted by a single tree or
even a shrub ; not a living creature was to be seen, and
the sun began already to throw a fiery veil over all
around, making the vicinity of the cooling element desirable. After a little more than half an hour's ride we
reached swampy ground, and began to make our way
through the water, often up to our knees on horseback.

      *   *   *   *   *

Then turning a little more to the north, and passing
still through deep water full of grass, and most fatiguing
for the horses, while it seemed most delightful to me after
my dry and dreary journey through this continent, we
reached another creek, called ' Dímbebér.' Here I was
so fortunate as to see two small boats, or ' mákara,' of
the Búdduma, as they are called by the Kanúri, or
Yédiná, as they call themselves, the famous pirates of
the Tsád. They were small flat boats, made of the light
and narrow wood of the ' fógo,' about 12 feet long, and
managed by two men each. As soon as the men saw us,
they pushed their boats off from the shore. They were
evidently in search of human prey ; and as we had seen
people from the neighbouring villages who had come
here to cut reeds to thatch their huts anew for the rainy
season, we went first to inform them of the presence of
these constant enemies of the inhabitants of these fertile
banks of the lagoon, that they might be on their guard ;

for they could not see them, owing to the quantity of tall reeds with which the banks and the neighbouring land was overgrown.

We then continued our watery march. The sun was by this time very powerful; but a very gentle cooling breeze came over the lagoon, and made the heat supportable. We had water enough to quench our thirst—indeed, more than we really wanted; for we might have often drunk with our mouth by stooping down a little on horseback, so deeply were we immersed. But the water was exceedingly warm, and full of vegetable matter. It is perfectly fresh, as fresh as water can be. It seems to have been merely from prejudice that people in Europe have come to the conclusion that this Central African basin must either have an outlet, or must be salt. For I can positively assert that it has no outlet, and that its water is perfectly fresh. Indeed, I do not see from whence saltness of the water should arise in a district in which there is no salt at all, and in which the herbage is so destitute of this element, that the milk of the cows and sheep fed on it is rather insipid, and somewhat unwholesome. Certainly in the holes around the lagoon, where the soil is strongly impregnated with natron, and which are only for a short time of the year in connection with the lake, the water, when in small quantity, must savour of the peculiar quality of the soil; but when these holes are full, the water in them likewise is fresh.

While we rode along these marshy, luxuriant plains, large herds of ' kelára ' started up, bounding over the rushes, and sometimes swimming, at others running, soon disappeared in the distance. This is a peculiar kind of antelope, which I have nowhere seen but in the immediate vicinity of the lake. In colour and size it resembles the roe, and has a white belly.

＊　　　　＊　　　　＊　　　　＊　　　　＊

Proceeding onwards, we reached about noon another creek, which is used occasionally by the Búdduma as a harbour, and is called ' Ngúlbeá.' We, however, found it empty, and only inhabited by ngurútus, or river-horses, which, indeed, live here in great numbers, snorting about in every direction, and by two species of crocodiles. In this quarter there are no elephants, for the very simple reason that they have no place of retreat during the night; for this immense animal (at least in . Africa) appears to be very sensible of the convenience of a soft couch in the sand, and of the inconvenience of mosquitoes too; wherefore it prefers to lie down on a spot a little elevated above the swampy ground, whither it resorts for its daily food. On the banks of the northern part of the Tsád, on the contrary, where a range of low sand-hills and wood encompasses the lagoon, we shall meet with immense herds of this animal.

26. TIMBUCTOO ENTERED.

H. BARTH,[*] 1853.

After a rather restless night, the day broke when I was at length to enter Timbúktu; but we had a good deal of trouble in performing this last short stage of our journey, deprived as we were of beasts of burden; for the two camels which the people had brought from the town in order to carry my boxes proved much too weak, and it was only after a long delay that we were able to procure eleven donkeys for the transport of all my luggage. Meanwhile the rumour of a traveller of importance having arrived had spread far and wide, and

[*] ' Travels in North and Central Africa.'

several inhabitants of the place sent a breakfast both for myself and my protector.

   *   *   *   *   *

 It was ten o'clock when our cavalcade at length put itself in motion, ascending the sandhills which rise close behind the village of Kábara, and which, to my great regret, had prevented my obtaining a view of the town from the top of our terrace. The contrast of this desolate scenery with the character of the fertile banks of the river which I had just left behind was remarkable. The whole tract bore decidedly the character of a desert, although the path was thickly lined on both sides with thorny bushes and stunted trees, which were being cleared away in some places in order to render the path less obstructed and more safe, as the Tawárek never fail to infest it, and at present were particularly dreaded on account of their having killed a few days previously three petty Tawáti traders on their way to A'rawán. It is from the unsafe character of this short road between the harbour and the town that the spot, about halfway between Kábara and Timbúktu, bears the remarkable name of ' Ur-immándes,' ' He does not hear,' meaning the place where the cry of the unfortunate victim is not heard from either side.

 Having traversed two sunken spots designated by especial names, where, in certain years when the river rises to an unusual height, as happened in the course of the same winter, the water of the inundation enters and occasionally forms even a navigable channel; and leaving on one side the talha tree of the Welí Sálah, covered with innumerable rags of the superstitious natives, who expect to be generously rewarded by their saint with a new shirt, we approached the town; but its dark masses of clay not being illuminated by bright sunshine, for the sky was thickly overcast and the atmosphere filled with

6

sand, were scarcely to be distinguished from the sand
and rubbish heaped all round; and there was no opportunity for looking attentively about, as a body of people
were coming towards us in order to pay their compli-
ments to the stranger and bid him welcome. This was
a very important moment, as, if they had felt the slightest
suspicion with regard to my character, they might easily
have prevented my entering the town at all, and thus
even endangered my life.

I therefore took the hint of A'lawáte, who recommended
me to make a start in advance in order to anticipate the
salute of these people who had come to meet us; and
putting my horse to a gallop, and gun in hand, I galloped
up to meet them, when I was received with many salaams.
But a circumstance occurred which might have proved
fatal, not only to my enterprise, but even to my own
personal safety, as there was a man among the group
who addressed me in Turkish, which I had almost entirely
forgotten, so that I could with difficulty make a suitable
answer to his compliment; but avoiding farther indis-
creet questions, I pushed on in order to get under safe
cover.

Having then traversed the rubbish which has accumulated round the ruined clay wall of the town, and left on
one side a row of dirty reed huts which encompass the
whole of the place, we entered the narrow streets and
lanes, or, as the people of Timbúktu say, the tijeráten,
which scarcely allowed two horses to proceed abreast.
But I was not a little surprised at the populous and
wealthy character which this quarter of the town, the
Sáne-Gúngu, exhibited, many of the houses rising to the
height of two stories, and in their façade evincing even
an attempt at architectural adornment. Thus, taking a
more westerly turn, and followed by a numerous troop

of people, we passed the house of the Sheikh El Bakáy, where I was desired to fire a pistol ; but, as I had all my arms loaded with ball, I prudently declined to do so, and left it to one of my people to do honour to the house of our host. We thus reached the house on the other side of the street which was destined for my residence, and I was glad when I found myself safely in my new quarters.

PART III.

THE CIRCUMNAVIGATION OF AFRICA.

INTRODUCTION.

THAT on maps up to the middle of the nineteenth century almost the whole interior of Central Africa should have been left blank, as 'unexplored territory,' strikes us perhaps as less strange than that the very outline of the continent, familiar to all of us from our earliest days, should have been unknown to the world less than five centuries ago. Yet even so late as that in the world's history there was no real evidence to show where Africa ended, or even whether it did not run on to join with some vast unknown continent which geographers, until the days of Captain Cook, loved to imagine in the unexplored southern ocean.

Of course, there was the famous story of the Phœnician expedition preserved by Herodotus to prove the contrary, if only it could be believed—and in modern times very many have believed it, by reason of that very part of the story which made Herodotus himself doubtful. For it is clear that anyone sailing from east to west south of the tropic of Capricorn must really have the sun almost all day to the north of him—that is, to his right—and it seems unlikely that anyone who did not know this should invent anything which would seem so improbable. But it must be remembered, on the other hand, that the later Greek geographers, who understood these things as well as we do, and who were, moreover, well aware that Africa stretched much further to the south than Herodotus, who thought it smaller than Europe, can have supposed, took little or no account of this story.

There is better reason for putting faith in the 'periplus'—that is, circumnavigation—of Hanno the Carthaginian. It is even said that his furthest point, the island of the gorillas, can be identified with an island at Sherboro, a little to the south of Sierra Leone. Others have thought that the mention of the high mountain which at night looked like a fire proves that Hanno must have gone still further, and seen the volcanic mountains of Fernando Po or the Cameroons. But if we suppose that the many other fires which alarmed his crew were merely due to the native custom of burning the dry grass (see 29 and 82), we need not assume another explanation for this particular fire, which may simply have been a conflagration far up the sides of a very high hill. And this would probably be the same as the Mount Sagres which the followers of Piedro de Cintra thought the highest cape they had ever seen. It is a little way to the north of the tenth parallel of latitude. If this be so, the wooded hills with the sweet smell would be Cape Verde, the gulf beyond them the Gambia, the crocodile river before them the Senegal, etc.

The name 'gorilla' which we derive from this ancient story is applied nowadays to the great man-like ape of West Central Africa (see 75). But what Hanno's gorillas were has been much questioned, some holding that they really were these apes, some that they were merely baboons, some that they actually belonged to a race, now extinct, of hairy human savages. Their skins are said to have been preserved at Carthage long after this voyage, which can hardly have happened later than the third century B.C., and it is odd if the Carthaginians, who certainly knew baboons, should not have recognised a baboon's skin.

It was not till the fifteenth century that the Portuguese, at the instigation of their famous ' Prince Henry the Navigator,' began the explorations which, extending gradually down the west coast of Africa, led at last to the rounding of the Cape and the discovery of a sea-route to India. It is curious that after nearly a century's efforts to reach it the Cape should have been passed unawares, and it seems strange that its discoverer should apparently have felt no pride in having done so much, for disappointment at not being able to do more. But the hope of reaching India was ever before the minds of the Portuguese, and this glory was reserved for Vasco da Gama, five years after Columbus had discovered the new world of the West. His famous journey, and those which succeeded it, of course made the Portuguese acquainted with the east coast of Africa, where they are still established long after most of the coast they discovered on the west has fallen to later comers—Dutch, French, English, and German.

The east coast, however, was not entirely new ground, as the Arabs had long since made settlements there, especially in the neighbourhood of Zanzibar. Beyond these the the Portugese reached a country which aroused the deepest interest in Europe—the Christian kingdom of Abyssinia. In the many-titled ruler of this mountain land, which had preserved its religion through all the Mohammedan conquests from the fall of the Roman Empire, they believed that Prester John—that is to say,

John the Presbyter or Priest, the mysterious Christian potentate whom the Middle Ages believed to bear rule somewhere in the East—had, after ages of invisibility, been found at last.

27. THE PHŒNICIAN EXPEDITION.*

? 600 B.C.

As to Libya, the case is clear,† seeing that it is encircled on all sides, except that which borders upon Asia, by the sea, as Necho, King of the Egyptians, was the first, so far as we know, to prove. For when he gave over digging the canal that ran from the Nile to the Arabian Gulf, he sent out certain Phœnicians in ships with orders to sail for the northern sea in the contrary direction by the Pillars of Hercules, and so to arrive at Egypt. The Phœnicians accordingly set out to sail the southern waters, starting from the Red Sea. When autumn came round they would put in to that point of the Libyan coast off which they found themselves, and sowing the land, await the harvest, and when they had reaped the corn sail on again. And after two years had thus gone by, in the third they rounded the Pillars of Hercules, and arrived in Egypt. And they told a tale which I do not believe, though another perhaps may, that as they were sailing round Libya they had the sun on their right. Thus was the extent of that region found out for the first time.

---

* Herodotus, iv. 42.

† *I.e.*, that Africa, as Herodotus thought, was much less extensive than Europe.

28. THE 'PERIPLUS' OF HANNO THE CARTHAGINIAN.*

? 500 B.C.

Putting to sea, we passed the Pillars of Hercules and sailed beyond them for the space of two days, when we founded our first colony, which we named Thymiaterion; there was a wide plain beneath it. Then voyaging to the west, we came to Soloeis, a promontory of Libya, thickly overgrown with trees.

There we founded a temple to Poseidon, and again went on to the east for the space of half a day, till we reached a lake near to the sea, full of reeds many and tall, and upon it were elephants and other wild beasts in great numbers feeding.

And when we had gone a day's journey beyond the lake, we founded settlements by the seaside under the names of Carian Castle and Gytte and Acra and Melitta and Arambys.

And sailing thence, we came to Lixus, a large river flowing out of Libya, by which the Lixites, a nomad folk, were feeding their flocks, whose friendship we gained, and abode with them for a season. Landward of them were unfriendly Ethiopians, inhabiting a land of wild beasts, broken up by high mountains. Out of these, we were told, the Lixus flows, and around them live men of a strange aspect, dwellers in caves, who, the Lixites say, can outstrip a horse in running.

We took some of the Lixites as interpreters, and coasted along a desert shore to the southward for two days, and again to the east for a day's journey. Here at

---

* Müller's ' Geographi Græci Minores.'

the head of a certain bay we found a small island five stades in circuit, which we colonized, naming it Cerne. We reckoned according to our voyage that it lay in a right line with Carthage, as the sail from Carthage to the Pillars, and the sail thence to Cerne, were alike.

From here we sailed up a large river, called Chretes, and reached a lake, in which were three islands larger than Cerne. From them we made one day's sail and came to the head of the lake, over which hung very high mountains, thronged with wild men, clad in the skins of beasts, who beat us off by throwing stones upon us, and so kept us from landing. And sailing thence, we came to another river, deep and wide, full of crocodiles and river-horses. . . . Thence for twelve days we sailed to the south, keeping near to the land, wherein at all points there were Ethiopians dwelling ; but they fled from us, and would not abide our approach, nor could their speech be understood even by the Lixites who were with us. But on the last of these days we anchored close in to high hills thickly covered with wood, and the trees were of divers kinds of wood that had a sweet smell. And when in two days we had sailed round them we found ourselves in a gulf of the sea exceeding large, on the further side of which inland was flat ground, and thence, when the night came, we saw fire going up on all sides at intervals, here a greater and there a less.

Here we watered our ships, and sailed onwards along the coast five days, until we came to a great bay which the interpreters called the Western Horn. In it was a large island, and on the island a lake with waters like the sea, and in it yet another island on which we landed, and saw, while it was day, nothing beside forest, but at night many fires burning, and heard a sound of flutes and a great rattling and clanging of cymbals and tabors.

Fear came upon us, and our soothsayers admonished us that we should avoid the island.

With haste we sailed away, and went on past a region which was on fire and full of the smell of incense, and from it torrents of fire were rushing into the sea. And the land could not be approached for the heat.

Hence too we sailed in haste, for we were afraid. And for four days, as we ran, we saw the land at night full of fire, and in the midst was a certain lofty fire, greater than the rest, which seemed to touch the stars. By day this was seen to be a very high mountain, the name of which is called The Chariot of the Gods.

From here, on the third day, when we had passed by streams of fire, we came to a bay called the Southern Horn. And at its head was an island like to the former one, having on it a lake, and in this was another island, thronged with wild men. Of these much the greater number were females, with shaggy bodies, whom the interpreters called Gorillas. Giving chase to them, we could catch none of the males, but all escaped, going easily upon the cliffs, and defending themselves with stones ; but we caught three females, who bit and scratched their captors and would not follow. So we killed them and flayed them, and brought the skins home to Carthage. For we sailed no further than this, as provisions failed us.

29. HANNO'S FIRST MODERN FOLLOWER.

PIEDRO DA CINTRA.* A.D. 1462.

The two Voyages of Cada Mosto to the Coast of Africa were followed by others, performed by the Portugueze.

* Astley's ' Collection of Voyages.' 1745.

Among the Ships that went, there were, in particular, two armed Caravels, sent by the King of Portugal.

They went to those two large and inhabited Islands near the Mouth of the said River, where, having landed, they ordered their Negros to speak to them, but they could not be understood by the People. Then they went up into the Land to see their Habitations, which were poor thatched Houses, in some whereof they found wooden Idols, which the Negros worshipped. Not being able to get any Information from these People, they sailed along the Coast, and came to the Mouth of a large River, which was between three and four Miles wide, and reckoned that it was about forty Miles distant from the Rio Grande. This River, he said, was called Besegue, from a Lord of that Name, who dwells near the Mouth of it.

And proceeding farther, they came up with a Cape, to which they gave the Name of Cape Verga. All the Coast, from Besegue River to this Cape, which is about an hundred and forty Miles in Length, is very hilly, and full of high Trees; which look beautiful at a great Distance.

Sailing along the Coast from Cape Verga, about eighty Miles, they met with another Cape, which, in the opinion of all the Seamen, was the highest they ever had seen; forming a sharp Point in the Middle of the Height thereof, like a Diamond. The whole Cape is covered with beautiful green Trees. They gave it the Name of Sagres, which they took from a Fortress built by the deceased Prince Don Enriquez, on Cape St. Vincent; and for this Reason it is called by the Portugueze Cape Sagres of Guinea.

The Sailors say that the Inhabitants are Idolaters, according to the Accounts they had of them; and that

they worship wooden Images, made in the Shape of Men,
to whom they offer Victuals as often as they eat or drink.
They are rather of a tawny Colour than black, with
Marks on their Faces and Bodies, made with a hot Iron.
They go naked; and for Breeches, wear the Barks of
Trees. . . .

The Inhabitants of this River have also large Alma-
dias, which carry from thirty to forty Men, who row
standing, without having their Oars fixed to any Thing;
as already observed. They have their Ears pierced with
Holes all round, in which they wear various Sorts of
Gold Rings. The Nose is likewise pierced, both in
Men and Women; who wear a Gold Ring in it, as our
Buffaloes do of other Metal, and take it out when at
Victuals. . . .

Having passed Cape Sagres, and ran along the Coast
about forty Miles farther, they came to the Mouth of
Rio de San Vincente, which is about four Miles wide;
and about five Miles thence, on the same Coast, there is
another River, called Rio Verde, larger in the Entrance
than the former. Both these Rivers were so named
by the King's Sailors belonging to the two Caravels.
The Country and Coast is very mountainous, but there
is safe Sailing and good Mooring. About twenty-four
Miles beyond the River Verde, they met with another
Cape, which they called Liedo; that is, Brisk, or Cheerful,
because the beautiful green Country about it seemed to
smile.

From Cape Liedo there runs a large Mountain for
about fifty Miles along the Coast, which is very high,
and covered with lofty green Trees; at the End whereof,
about eight Miles in the Sea, there are three Islands, the
largest not above ten or twelve Miles in Circumference.
To these they gave the Name of Saluezze; and to the

Mountain, Sierra Leona, on Account of the Roaring of Thunder heard from the Top, which is always buried in Clouds.

Sailing on beyond Sierra Leona, there follows a low Country and Shore full of Sand-Banks, which run into the Sea ; and about thirty Miles from the Mountain, there is another large River, near three Miles wide at the Entrance. To this they gave the Name of River Roxo, because the Water looked red ; and farther on, there lies a Cape, which, appearing red, they called it Cape Roxo : As from this Cape they gave the Name of Roxa to a small uninhabited Island about eight Miles distant. From this Island (which is but ten Miles from the River also) the North Pole appeared the Height of a Man above the Sea.

    ✻   ✻   ✻   ✻   ✻

About seventy Miles beyond St. Ann's Cape, there is another River, to which they gave the Name of the River of Palms, from the Plenty of those Trees there. The Mouth, though wide enough, is full of Sand-Banks and Shoals, which make the entrance very dangerous. About seventy Miles farther on, there is another small River, which they called Rio de Fumi : because at the Time of their Discovering it they saw nothing but Smoke along this Coast, made by the Inhabitants ; and about twenty-four Miles beyond, there is a Cape which runs a great Way into the Sea, over which stands a high Mountain, whence they named it Capo del Monte. About sixty Miles farther on, there is another Cape, but small, with a little Mountain thereon, to which they gave the Name of Capo Cortese, or Misurado. The first Night after their Arrival here they saw many Fires among the Trees, made by the Negros, who had Sight of the Ships, and never had seen such Things before.

Beyond this Cape, about sixteen Miles close to the Shore, there is a large Wood full of green Trees, to which they gave the Name of St. Mary's Wood, or Grove. Behind this the Caravels came to an Anchor ; and some Almadias, with two or three Negros all naked, advanced with sharp-pointed Poles in their Hands, which, to the Europeans, seemed Darts : Others had small Knives, and but two Targets made of Skin, and three Bows among them all. Their Ears were all pierced, and the Nose likewise, in which they hung something like Men's Teeth. The Interpreters spoke to them, but could not understand a Word of their Language. Three of these Negros having ventured on board a Caravel, the Portugueze kept one, and let the other two go : for the King of Portugal had ordered them, in case the Interpreters could not understand the Inhabitants of the last country they should discover, that they should, by fair Means or Force, bring away one of the Natives : in Hopes either that some of the many Negros who were in Portugal would understand his Language ; or that, by learning the Portugueze Tongue, he might be able to give an Account of his Country. . . .

Whatever Intelligence the King received from him, was kept a Secret ; excepting that, among other Things, he had declared there were Unicorns in his Country. The King kept this Negro for some Months, and having caused several Curiosities of his Kingdom to be shewn him, gave him Cloaths, and with great Civility sent him by a Caravel back to his own Country.

30. DISCOVERY OF THE CONGO MOUTH.

DIEGO CAM,* 1484.

Henceforward the king would no more allow the captains whom he sent out for the discovery of that coast to set up wooden crosses in conspicuous places, . . . but commanded that they should prepare a stone column of twice the height of a man, bearing the royal arms of the kingdom, and on the sides an inscription in Latin and Portuguese, declaring what king had caused that land to be discovered, and at what time and by what captain that pillar had been raised; and at the top there was to be a stone cross soldered on with lead.

And the first discoverer to raise such a pillar was Diego Cam, a knight of his household, in the year 1484, who, having already put in to Mina, as to a place where he might obtain supplies for a voyage, sailed thence to the Cape of Lopo Gonsalvez, which lies under the first degree of south latitude. After rounding this cape, and likewise Cabo de Catherina, the last land which was dis-covered in the time of King Alfonso, he came to a notable river, at the mouth of which, on the south side, he set up a pillar, signifying that he took possession of all that coast, which lay behind him, in the name of the king. By reason of this pillar, which was named after St. George, because the king held that saint in peculiar veneration, this river was long called Padrão; but they now call it Congo, because it flows through a kingdom of that name, discovered by Diego Cam on this voyage, although by the natives the river is properly called Zaire.

It is more to be regarded for its stream than its name,

* From the 'Asia' of J. De Barros, 1550.

for at the season when there is winter in those countries it runs into the sea with such strength that the fresh water from it is traced even twenty miles from the coast. When Diego Cam had set up the pillar, and saw the force which the river displayed in its outflow and stream, it was clear to him that on so great a river there must be many settlements; and when he ascended it a little way, he perceived that many people showed themselves on its banks, all of them very black, with woolly hair, as he had met with them all along the coast above.

31. DISCOVERY OF THE CAPE OF GOOD HOPE.

BARTHOLOMEW DIAS,* 1487.

Nor were they content with setting up the pillars that they brought with them at such intervals along the coast as seemed good to them, but others also were erected at remarkable places, as, for instance, the first pillar, named after St. James, at a place to which they gave the name of Serra Parda, and which lies under the twenty-fourth parallel, a hundred and twenty miles beyond the last pillar which Diego Cam set up. In like manner they named the capes, bays and tracts of land which they discovered, either in honour of the day on which they arrived there, or for some other reason. For instance, the bay which we now call Voltas, to which they gave this name, Angra das Voltas, because of the many tacks they had to make when they then sailed by it. At this point storms, against which they could not make sail, delayed Bartholomew Dias for five whole days. The bay lies under the twenty-ninth degree of south latitude.

* From De Barros.

This same tempest, when they had again put out to sea, drove them before it for three days, and because their ships were small, and the seas now grew colder and of a different character from those in the latitudes of Guinea, they gave themselves up for lost, although even off the coast of Spain, too, the waves in time of storm are very cold.   But when the storm which so dismayed them abated, they thought, by setting an easterly course, to make the land, supposing that the coast still kept the general direction of north to south which they had hitherto found it to hold.   But when they saw that, though they steered thus for several days, they did not strike land, they altered their course to north, and so arrived at a bay which they named Vaqueiros, on account of the numerous cattle tended by herdsmen which they saw upon the shore.   With these people, for want of any interpreter who might have understood them, they could not come to speech, all the less because they, as men dismayed at so strange an adventure, drove their cattle into the country, so that our men learnt nothing about them, except that they were blacks, and had curly hair, like the people of Guinea.   As they went forward along the coast, and now in a direction wholly new, at which the leaders rejoiced greatly, they came to a small island, which lies under the thirty-third degree of south latitude.   There they set up a pillar, named after the cross that gave its name to the island, which lies rather more than half a mile from the mainland, and is called by many Penedo das Fontes, because there are two springs of water upon it.

Here the crews, who were weary of the storms which beset them, and afraid besides, all with one voice raised loud complaints, and demanded to be led no further.   It was time, they said, now that their provisions were

7

spoiling, to turn back and look for the ship which they
had left behind with their supplies, and which was
already at such a distance behind them that they were
all like to be starved even if they reached it, much more
if they were to go on. Enough had been done for one
voyage in the discovery of so vast a region, and the most
important news that could be obtained from that exploration was already obtained, inasmuch as they had learnt
that the land ran almost uninterruptedly to the east.
From this it was plain that behind him lay some great
promontory, and to turn back and look for it were the
better counsel.

To satisfy complaints so numerous, Bartholomew Dias
landed with the captains, officers, and some of the most
respected of the seamen, and administering to them an
oath, bade them say truly what, in their judgment, their
duty to the king required them to do. And when all,
for the reasons aforesaid and others equally good, agreed
that they ought to return homewards, he put their
decision into the form of a document, which they all
signed. But as it was his own wish to go forwards, and
he had yielded thus far only because compelled thereto
by his duty and by the instructions of the king, who had
therein enjoined him to take counsel on all occasions of
importance with the principal persons that accompanied
him, he besought them all, when it came to signing their
decision, that they would consent to travel yet two or
three days along the coast, and if in that time they found
no reason for sailing further, then to turn back. This
was granted to him. But within the three days for
which he had begged nothing more important befel than
their arrival at a river, which lies under the parallel of
thirty-two degrees and two thirds, twenty-five miles
beyond the Island of the Cross. And as João Infante,

captain of the St. Pantelão, was the first to set foot on
shore, the river received the name Infante, which it
still bears.   Here they turned back, as the seamen
renewed their clamours.   When they were again arrived
at the Island of the Cross, and Bartholomew Dias was
obliged to bid farewell to the pillar which he had there
erected, it was with such grief and emotion as if he were
there leaving a son in perpetual banishment.   It came
into his mind how great perils himself and all his company had encountered in coming from so great a distance
only to reach this goal, since God had withheld from
them their chief desire.

Proceeding now on their way, they came in sight of
that great and notable Cape which had for so many centuries remained hidden, in such wise that with it, when
at last it came to light, not itself only but another new
world was discovered.   To it Bartholomew Dias and his
company gave the name Stormy, in remembrance of the
dangers and tempests which had beset them in the
rounding of it; but when they returned home, the king,
Don John, gave it another and fairer name, calling it the
Cape of Good Hope, because it awoke the hope that
India, so much desired and so long sought, would be
found at last.

32. THE CAPE OF GOOD HOPE.

C. J. BUNBURY,* 1848.

As we approached from the south-west, we had an
excellent view of the fine mountainous line of coast
running down from Table Bay to the Cape of Good
Hope (properly so called), and it was with great interest
that I looked for the first time upon the continent of

* 'Journal of a Residence at the Cape.' (Murray, 1848.)

Africa. The whole of this line of coast is very bold and
high : the mountains rising abruptly from the sea, steep
and rugged and bare, in successive ledges, and massy
beds of rock, with little appearance of vegetation, their
crests rough and craggy, but not shooting up into those
sharp peaks which give such a peculiar character to the
coast of Brazil. They reminded us of some of the lower
secondary ranges of the Alps.

As we ran in pretty near to the shore, and the day
was beautifully clear, we saw these mountains to great
advantage, with the noonday light on their crags and
projections, and the deep furrows of their steep sides
thrown into dark shade, while the surf beat furiously on
their bases. There was scarcely a tinge of verdure on
them, all that was not bare rock had the brown hue of
parched and withered vegetation, and it was not till we
were under the hill called the Lion's Rump (which
bounds the bay on the south-west) that I saw a few
gardens and plantations relieving the barrenness of the
scene.

The famous Table Mountain was a conspicuous object,
being apparently the highest summit of the whole range;
but in this point of view it does not show the tabular
form for which it is noted, reminding one rather (in its
general outline as seen from a distance) of Salisbury
Crags, near Edinburgh.

As we opened the bay, the picturesque mountains of
Stellenbosch and Hottentots' Holland were seen far off
in the background. Long ranges of sandhills extended
along the shore northward of the bay, where the English
forces landed when they took the Cape in 1806, and
behind these appeared low mountains of a rounded form.

About five p.m. we came to anchor in Table Bay.
The appearance of Cape Town and the mountains behind

it seen from hence was pretty much what I had been led to expect from the prints of them which I had seen, for the principal features are so simple and strongly marked that it would be difficult not to catch the likeness in some degree. The town, standing on nearly flat ground, makes no very conspicuous figure. Immediately behind it, like a huge wall, rises the Table Mountain, so strongly characterized by its long and level top and its precipitous sides that it can never be mistaken. It has been very aptly compared to a part of the wall of a fortress with two bastions projecting beyond the general line of its front.

Adjoining to this, on the left as viewed from the bay, is the bold and rugged peak called the Devil's Mountain; on the right, a lower but very conspicuous rocky summit, known as the Lion's Head; and the long round-backed hill, running out nearly northward from this last, bears the name of the Lion's Rump. In fact, these two together, when viewed from the south-west and from some distance, have a rude resemblance to the figure of a couchant lion.

33. VASCO DA GAMA* ROUNDS THE CAPE.

1497.

In the name of God. Amen!

In the year 1497 King Dom Manuel, the first of that name in Portugal, despatched four vessels to make discoveries and go in search of spices. Vasco da Gama was the captain-major of these vessels; Paulo da Gama, his brother, commanded one of them, and Nicolau Coelho another.

* 'Journal of his First Voyage.' Translated by E. G. Ravenstein. (Hakluyt Society, 1898.)

[Lisbon to the Cape Verde Islands.]

We left Restello on Saturday, July 8, 1497. May
God our Lord permit us to accomplish this voyage in
His service. Amen!

On the following Saturday [July 15] we sighted the
Canaries, and in the night passed to the lee of Lançarote.
During the following night, at break of day [July 16] we
made the Terra Alta, where we fished for a couple of
hours, and in the evening, at dusk, we were off the Rio
do Ouro.

The fog during the night grew so dense that Paulo
da Gama lost sight of the captain-major, and when day
broke [July 17] we saw neither him nor the other vessels.
We therefore made sail for the Cape Verde islands, as
we had been instructed to do in case of becoming separated.

*   *   *   *   *

On Thursday, August 3, we left in an easterly direction. On August 18, when about 200 leagues from
Samtiagua, going south, the captain-major's mainyard
broke, and we lay to under foresail and lower mainsail
for two days and a night. On the 22nd of the same
month, when going S. by W., we saw many birds
resembling herons. On the approach of night they flew
vigorously to the S.S.E., as if making for the land. On
the same day, being then quite 800 leagues out at sea
[i.e., reckoning from S. Thiago], we saw a whale. . . .

On Wednesday, November 1, the day of All Saints,
we perceived many indications of the neighbourhood of
land, including gulf-weed, which grows along the coast.

On Saturday, the 4th of the same month, a couple
of hours before break of day, we had soundings in
110 fathoms, and at nine o'clock we sighted the land.

We then drew near to each other, and having put on our gala clothes, we saluted the captain-major by firing our bombards, and dressed the ships with flags and standards. In the course of the day we tacked so as to come close to the land ; but as we failed to identify it, we again stood out to sea.

[THE BAY OF ST. HELENA.]

On Tuesday [November 7] we returned to the land, which we found to be low, with a broad bay opening into it. The captain-major sent Pero d'Alenquer in a boat to take soundings and to search for good anchoring ground. The bay was found to be very clean, and to afford shelter against all winds except those from the N.W. It extended east and west, and we named it Santa Helena.

On Wednesday [November 8] we cast anchor in this bay, and we remained there eight days, cleaning the ships, mending the sails, and taking in wood. . . .

The inhabitants of this country are tawny-coloured. Their food is confined to the flesh of seals, whales, and gazelles, and the roots of herbs. They are dressed in skins. . . .

Their numerous dogs resemble those of Portugal, and bark like them. The birds of the country, likewise, are the same as in Portugal, and include cormorants, gulls, turtle-doves, crested larks, and many others. The climate is healthy and temperate, and produces good herbage.

On the day after we had cast anchor, that is to say on Thursday [November 9], we landed with the captain-major, and made captive one of the natives, who was small of stature like Sancho Mexia. This man had been gathering honey in the sandy waste, for in this country the bees deposit their honey at the foot of the mounds around the bushes. He was taken on board the captain-major's ship, and being placed at table he ate of all we ate. On the following day the captain-major had him well dressed and sent ashore.

On the following day [November 10] fourteen or fifteen natives came to where our ships lay. The captain-major landed and showed them a variety of merchandise, with the view of finding out whether such things were to be found in their country. This merchandise included cinnamon, cloves, seed-pearls, gold, and many other things; but it was evident that they had no knowledge whatever of such articles, and they were consequently given round bells and tin rings. This happened on Friday, and the like took place on Saturday.

On Sunday [November 12] about forty or fifty natives made their appearance. . . .

On that day Fernão Velloso, who was with the captain-major, expressed a great desire to be permitted to accompany the natives to their houses, so that he might find out how they lived and what they ate. The captain-major yielded to his importunities, and allowed him to accompany them; and when we returned to the captain-major's vessel to sup, he went away with the negroes. Soon after they had left us they caught a seal; and when they came to the foot of a hill in a barren place they roasted it, and gave some of it to Fernão Velloso, as also some of the roots which they eat. After this meal they expressed a desire that he should not accompany them any further, but return to the vessels. When Fernão Velloso came abreast of the vessels he began to shout, the negroes keeping in the Bush.

We were still at supper; but when his shouts were heard the captain-major rose at once, and so did we others, and we entered a sailing-boat. The negroes then

began running along the beach, and they came as quickly
up with Fernão Velloso as we did; and when we endeavoured to get him into the boat they threw their
assegais, and wounded the captain-major and three or
four others. All this happened because we looked upon
these people as men of little spirit, quite incapable of
violence, and had therefore landed without first arming
ourselves. We then returned to the ships.

[Rounding the Cape.]

At daybreak of Thursday, November 16, having
careened our ships and taken in wood, we set sail. At
that time we did not know how far we might be abaft
the Cape of Good Hope. Pero d'Alenquer thought the
distance about thirty leagues; but he was not certain,
for on his return voyage [when with B. Dias] he had
left the Cape in the morning and had gone past this bay
with the wind astern, whilst on the outward voyage he
had kept at sea, and was therefore unable to identify the
locality where we now were. We therefore stood out
towards the S.S.W., and late on Saturday [November 18]
we beheld the Cape. On that same day we again stood
out to sea, returning to the land in the course of the
night. On Sunday morning, November 19, we once
more made for the Cape; but were again unable to
round it, for the wind blew from the S.S.W., whilst the
Cape juts out towards the S.W. We then again stood
out to sea, returning to the land on Monday night. At
last, on Wednesday [November 22], at noon, having the
wind astern, we succeeded in doubling the Cape, and
then ran along the coast.

34. A SHORT ACCOUNT OF ABYSSINIA.

FATHER JEROME LOBO,* 1622.

The original of the Abyssins, like that of all other nations, is obscure and uncertain. The tradition generally received derives them from Cham, the son of Noah, and they pretend, however improbably, that from his time till now, the legal succession of their kings hath never been interrupted, and that the supreme power hath always continued in the same family. An authentic genealogy traced up so high could not but be extremely curious, and with good reason might the Emperors of Abyssinia boast themselves the most illustrious and ancient family in the world. But there are no real grounds for imagining that Providence has vouchsafed them so distinguishing a protection, and from the wars with which this empire hath been shaken in these latter ages, we may justly believe that, like all others, it has suffered its revolutions, and that the history of the Abyssins is corrupted with fables.

This empire is known by the name of the kingdom of Prester John. For the Portuguese, having heard such wonderful relations of an ancient and famous Christian state called by that name in the Indies, imagined it could be none but this of Æthiopia. Many things concurred to make them of this opinion; there was no Christian kingdom or state in the Indies of which all was true which they heard of this land of Prester John, and there was none in the other parts of the world who was a Christian separated from the Catholick Church but what was known except this kingdom of Æthiopia. It has

* Pinkerton's 'Voyages,' 1814.

therefore passed for the kingdom of Prester John since the time that it was discovered by the Portuguese in the reign of King John II.

35. THE PRISON OF PRESTER JOHN'S SONS.

FATHER FRANCISCO ALVAREZ,* 1520-1527.

The above-mentioned valley reaches to the mountain where they put the sons of the Prester John. These are like banished men; as it was revealed to King Abraham . . . that all his sons should be shut up in a mountain, and that none should remain except the firstborn, the heir, and that this should be done for ever to all the sons of the Prester of the country and his successors, because if this was not so done there would be great difficulty in the country on account of its greatness, and they would rise up and seize parts of it, and would not obey the heir, and would kill him. He being frightened at such a revelation, and reflecting where such a mountain could be found, it was again told him in revelation to order his country to be searched, and to look at the highest mountains, and that mountain on which they saw wild goats on the rocks looking as if they were going to fall below was the mountain on which the princes were to be shut up. He ordered it to be done as it had been revealed to him, and they found this mountain, which stands above this valley, to be the one which the revelation mentioned, round the foot of which a man has to go a journey of two days; and it is of this kind: a rock cut like a wall, straight from the top to the bottom; a man going at the foot of it, and looking upwards, it seems that the sky rests upon it. They say that it has three entrances or

* 'Portuguese Embassy to Abyssinia.' (Hakluyt Society, 1881.)

gates in three places, and no more. I saw one of these
here in this country, and I saw it in this manner. We
were going from the sea to the court, and a young man,
a servant of the Prester, whom they call a *calacem*, was
guiding us, and he did not know the country well; and
we wished to lodge in a town, and they would not
receive us; this belonged to a sister of Prester John.
The night had not yet advanced much, and he began
travelling, telling us to follow him, and that he would
get us lodgings. And because he travelled fast on a
mule and on a small path, I told one Lopo da Gama to
ride in sight of the *calacem*, and that I would keep him in
sight, and the Ambassador and the other people would
ride in sight of me. And the night closed in when we
were quite a league from the road towards the mountain
of the princes, and there came forth from all the villages
so many people throwing stones at us that they were
near killing us, and they made us disperse in three or
four directions. The Ambassador had remained in the
rear, and he turned back, and others who were about in
the middle of the party started off in another direction;
and someone there was who dismounted from his mule
and fled in panic. Lopo da Gama and I could not turn
back, so we went forward and reached another town,
which was still better prepared on account of the noise
which they heard behind in the other towns. Here
many stones rained upon us, and the darkness was like
having no eyes. In order that they might not throw
stones at me by hearing the mule's steps, I dismounted,
and gave the mule to my slave. God was pleased that
an honourable man came up to me and asked me who
I was. I told him that I was a *gaxia neguz*—that is to
say, 'a king's stranger.' This man was very tall, and I
say honourable, because he treated me well; and he took

my head under his arm, for I did not reach any higher, and so he conducted me like the bellows of a bagpipe player, saying ' *Atefra, atefra,*' which means, ' Do not be afraid, do not be afraid.'   He took me with the mule and the slave until he brought me into a vegetable garden which surrounded his house.   Inside this garden he had a quantity of poles stuck up one against another, and in the midst of these poles he had a clean resting-place like a hut, into which he put me.   As it seemed to me that I was in safety, I ordered a light to be lit ; and when they saw the light they rained stones on the hut, and when I put out the light the stone-throwing ceased.   The host, as soon as he left me, returned at the noise, and then remained an hour without coming.   Whilst he was away, Lopo da Gama heard me, and broke through the bushes and came to me.   On this the host came and said, ' Be quiet, do not be afraid,' and ordered a candle to be lit and to kill two fowls, and he gave us bread and wine and a hospitable welcome according to his power.   Next day, in the morning, the host took me by the hand and led me to his house, as far as a game of ball, where there were many trees of an inferior kind, and very thick, by which it was concealed as by a wall, and between them was a door, which was locked, and before this door was an ascent to the cliff.   This host said to me : ' Look here, if any of you were to pass inside this door, there would be nothing for it but to cut off his feet and his hands, and put out his eyes, and leave him lying there ; and you must not put the blame on those who would do this, neither would you be in fault, but those who brought you hither.   We, if we did not do this, we should pay with our lives, because we are the guardians · of this door.'

36. EPIPHANY IN ABYSSINIA.

J. THEODORE BENT,* 1893.

Shortly after our return to Asmara was the day of Epiphany, for the Abyssinians, like the Greeks, follow the old calendar, and their festivities consequently fall twelve days later than they do with us. We looked forward to this ceremony with intense interest, for it is the second biggest festival in the Ethiopian Church, second only to the great day of *mascal,* or the blessing of the cross, which takes place in September. It is a sort of vast lustration or baptism of the whole Ethiopian race, a day of great festivity, both social and religious; the cross is publicly baptized in a neighbouring stream, and to celebrate this event all the magnificent ritual of the Abyssinian Church is brought into play.

Very early in the morning the ceremony began. As soon as the sun was up we started for the scene of action, across the plain to the stream where the cross was to be baptized. Hoar frost covered the ground, and the air was keen but intensely invigorating. Already the people were beginning to assemble, pouring in from all sides, dressed in their smartest and gayest; at the old church in the village the priests and acolytes had already assembled, and were preparing for the procession. I do not think any religious procession I have ever seen impressed me so much as this line of dusky Ethiopians, rich in the display of their quaint ritual and costumes, which have here survived from the earliest days of Christianity.

At the head of the procession marched a man carrying a heavy umbrella, made of purple velvet, and covered

* ' Sacred City of the Ethiopians.' (Longmans, 1893.)

with silver ornaments; on the top was a cross and
massive object in silver, and the edges were fringed
with the long, tongueless bells, which is so favourite a
form of decoration in Abyssinia.   There were many
similar umbrellas in the procession—some, however, only
plain scarlet, and some only white.   However, as seen
from a distance, the most striking feature of this
Epiphany procession is its wealth of umbrellas, reminding one of the Assyrian tablets in the British Museum,
and other representations of ancient Eastern display,
which seems invariably to have revelled in a wealth of
umbrellas.

There were many acolytes, too, wearing massive mitres
or imperial crowns of brass, which would have enveloped
their whole heads had they not stuffed them with Turkey
red to keep them in their place.   The priests walked in
their white robes and white turbans—in one hand a
sistrum, which they rattled vigorously, and in the other
a brass-headed crutch.   About the middle of the procession walked a priest, entirely enveloped in purple
cloaks, so that not even his face was visible; and on the
top of his head he carried the sacred picture of Asmara,
covered with a cloth, so that vulgar eyes might not rest
upon it.   Over twenty of these oddly-decorated indi-
viduals, gorgeous in colour, some carrying umbrellas,
some silver crosses, some sacred books, wound their way
towards the stream.

About ten yards from the water was pitched a large
tent of red cloth, erected for the benefit of the priests
who wished to change their robes unobserved.   When
all were assembled on the bank, the cross and a large
brass basin were placed in the midst, and the service
began, the first portion of which consisted in reading out
of large books, held by acolytes, the gospels and portions

of Scripture appointed, the only part of which we could understand being the long genealogy of Christ, with So-and-so, the son of So-and-so, so oft repeated. During the reading burnt incense was wafted around from magnificent brass censers. . . .

The second portion of the service consisted of the dance of the priests. Dancing in the Abyssinian Church is traditionally supposed to have been derived from the fact that David danced before the ark, though I am more inclined to believe that the steps and the music have both been handed down from pagan times, and that the excuse of David has been invented to maintain this favourite and really graceful and solemn form of worship amongst them.

These religious dances, in steps, tune, and rhythm, forcibly reminded us of what a Greek chorus must have been round the altar of Dionysus. The cross and the brass basin have taken the place of the altar; the frankincense is there, and the singing and chanting are carried on in the form of a dialogue, as if one priest was announcing to another some good news which prompted hilarity; the black-faced, bare-legged priests, with white turbans and red velvet cloaks, a *sistrum* in one hand, and a crutch in the other, waved to and fro in the mazy dance, whilst boys beat the drums to regulate the time. The figures seemed to us something between a minuet and a quadrille. Every step was studied and graceful, as they changed over from side to side, shaking their rattles and waving their crutches, chanting the while in low and decidedly sweet tones. This performance continued for an hour, and we grew somewhat weary, but not so the Abyssinians.

PART IV.

THE NIGER.

INTRODUCTION.

THE mouth of the Niger, or river of the Blacks, the second of the two great African rivers whose names have come down to us from antiquity, was for centuries shrouded in as deep a mystery as that which hung over the sources of the Nile. None could discover whence the Nile came, none could discover whither the Niger went. The problem might have been easier had any-one been sure in what direction the river, during the known part of its course, was flowing ; but, unhappily, even this apparently simple point was long a matter of uncertainty. If we are to hold with some geographers of note that the great river in the land of the Pygmies to which the Nasamonians penetrated, and which, because of the crocodiles in it, some suspected to be the Nile itself (see 37), was in reality the Niger, then the Nasamonians must have made, without knowing it, a geographical discovery which waited more than two thousand years for its confirmation.

For the Niger of the ancient geographers is very vaguely described, and the learned men of medieval times, though they were rightly informed as to the existence of the large river beyond the desert, in the neighbourhood of the mysterious city Timbuctoo, knew

so little of its course that they were inclined to represent
it (see 38) as coming from some lake in the interior, and
flowing, not as in reality from west to east, but from
east to west. And this mistake was made the more
natural by the Portuguese discoveries of large rivers
running into the Atlantic, among which the huge mouth
of the Gambia in particular, until exploration had proved
it to belong to a comparatively short river, seemed only
a fitting outlet to the mighty Niger. It was not until
the closing years of the eighteenth century that the
British traveller, Mungo Park, making his way across
from the west coast, arrived in a state of exhaustion,
and with a horse too weak to carry him, at Segu, and
proved with certainty that the river ran from west to
east—that is, towards the middle of the continent. And
this only made the question of its outlet the more per-
plexing. Some thought that, instead of beginning in a
great lake, it ended in one. But Park held that the
waters of so strong a stream must certainly at last find
a way to the sea.

It can hardly be doubted that the first person to come
near the solution of the mystery was Mungo Park himself, who set out again ten years later to solve it or, as
unhappily it turned out, 'to die on the Niger.' For,
although the last tidings from him were sent from San-
sandig, a little to the east of Segu, and therefore only a
little further down the river than the point where he had
first sighted it, twenty years later it was discovered that
he had succeeded in descending the stream as far as
Bussa, which lies in about 10° 30' of N. latitude, and is
therefore only some 300 miles from the coast of the
Bight of Benin, where, as we now know, the river runs
out in a multitude of channels. But here Park was
killed, and his journals irretrievably lost, and with them

no doubt the key to the truth. Ten years after his
death, Tuckey's ill-fated expedition (see 61 and 62)
started to ascend the Congo in the hope and expectation
that, as Park himself had believed, it would turn out to
be the mouth of the Niger.

But within another ten years such theories were dis-
pelled for ever, and when Clapperton, starting from the
Guinea coast, had succeeded in crossing the river below
Bussa, no doubt could remain as to its southerly flow,
and as to the part of the ocean into which it discharged.
Clapperton died of fever in the midst of his explorations,
and the glory of actually tracing the river from Bussa to
the sea fell to the brothers Lander, the elder of whom
had been Clapperton's faithful companion, and neither of
whom survived the labours of their expedition by more
than a few years.

Their narrative, and the vivid description (42) of the
Benin River written about two hundred years ago by a
correspondent of the famous Bosman, who had certainly
no idea that he was living near the outlet of the great
Timbuctoo stream, will make it easy to understand why,
while the delta of the Nile has been the home of civilization from the earliest times, that of the Niger has been
the abode of fever and barbarism down to the present
day. The mosquitoes of which the Dutchman com-
plains are thought by some scientific men to have a
closer connection with the fever than he can have suspected. But it must always be remembered that the
Niger, which has quite recently become the scene of so
much English and French rivalry, has not everywhere
the deadly climate that prevails at its mouths, and that
the races which dwell along its banks higher up are of a
far higher character than the debased dwellers in the
delta.

37. NILE OR NIGER?

HERODOTUS, B.C. 450.*

Thus the river Nilus is found still to continue the space of four months' journey by land and water (less than in which time it is not possible for a man to come from Elephantina to the Automolians), taking his course and stream from the west part of the world, and falling of the sun.

Howbeit, in this place I purpose to recite a story told me by certain of the Cyreneans, who, fortuning to take a voyage to the oracle of Ammon, came in talk with Etearchus, King of the Ammonians, where by course of speech they fell at length to discourse and comment of Nilus, the head whereof was unsearchable, and not to be known. In which place Etearchus made mention of a certain people called Nasamones, of the country of Africa, inhabiting the quicksands, and all the coast that lieth to the east. Certain of these men coming to the court of Etearchus, and reporting divers strange and wonderful things of the deserts and wild chases of Africa, they chanced at length to tell of certain young gentlemen of their country, issued of the chief and most noble families of all their nation, who, being at a reasonable age, very youthful and valiant, determined in a bravery to go seek strange adventures, as well other as also this.

Five of them, being assigned thereto by lot, put themselves in voyage to go and search and descry the wilderness and desert places of Africa, to the end they might see more, and make further report thereof than ever any that had attempted the same. For the sea-coast of Africa,

* Englished by B. R., 1584: edited by A. Lang. (David Nutt, 1888.)

pointing to the North Pole, many nations do inhabit, beginning from Egypt, and continuing to the promontory named Soloes, wherein Africa hath his end and bound. All the places above the sea are haunted with wild and savage beasts, being altogether void and desolate, pestered with sand, and exceeding dry.

These gentlemen travellers, having made sufficient provision of water and other viands necessary for their journey, first of all passed the countries that were inhabited, and next after that came into the wild and waste regions amongst the caves and dens of fierce and untamed beasts, through which they held on their way to the west part of the earth. In which manner, after they had continued many days' journey, and travelled over a great part of the sandy countries, they came at length to espy certain fair and goodly trees growing in a fresh and pleasant meadow, whereunto incontinently making repair, and tasting the fruit that grew thereon, they were suddenly surprised and taken short by a company of little dwarfs, far under the common pitch and stature of men, whose tongue the gentlemen knew not, neither was their speech understood of them. Being apprehended, they were led away over sundry pools and meres into a city, where all the inhabitants were of the same stature and degree with those that had taken them, and of colour swart and black. Fast by the side of this city ran a swift and violent river, flowing from the west to the east, wherein were to be seen very hideous and terrible serpents called crocodiles.

To this end drew the talk of Etearchus, King of the Ammonians, save that he added besides how the Nasamonian gentlemen returned home to their own country (as the Cyreneans made recount), and how the people also of the city whither they were brought were all conjurers,

and given to the study of the Black Art. The flood
that had his passage by the city Etearchus supposed to
be the river Nilus.

38. MEDIEVAL IDEAS OF THE COURSE OF THE NIGER.

LEO AFRICANUS,* 1525.

This land of Negros hath a mighty river, which,
taking his name of the region, is called Niger. This
river taketh his original from the east out of a certain
desert called by the aforesaid Negros *Sen*. Others will
have this river to spring out of a certain lake, and so to
run westward till it exonerateth itself into the Ocean Sea.
Our cosmographers affirm that the said river of Niger
is derived out of Nilus, which they imagine for some
certain space to be swallowed up of the earth, and yet
at last to burst forth into such a lake as is before mentioned.   Some others are of opinion that this river
beginneth westward to spring out of a certain mountain,
and so running east, to make at length a huge lake ;
which verily is not like to be true, for they usually sail
westward from Tombuto to the kingdom of Guinea—
yea, and to the land of Melli also—both which in respect
of Tombuto are situate to the west.   Neither hath the
said land of Negros any kingdoms comparable for beautiful and pleasant soil unto those which adjoin unto the
banks of Niger.   And here it is to be noted that
(according to the opinion of our cosmographers) that
land of Negros by which Nilus is said to run (namely,
that part of the world which stretcheth eastward even to
the Indian Sea, some northerly parcel whereof abutteth

* ' History of Africa.'   (Hakluyt Society, 1896.)

upon the Red Sea, to wit, the country which lieth without the Gulf of Arabia) is not to be called any member or portion of Africa, and that for many reasons, which are to be found in the process of this history set down more at large. The said country is called by the Latins *Æthiopia*. From thence come certain religious friars seared or branded on the face with a hot iron, who are to be seen almost over all Europe, and specially at Rome. These people have an emperor, which they call *Prete Gianni*, the greater part of that land being inhabited with Christians.

39. MUNGO PARK REACHES THE NIGER.*

JULY 20, 1796.

Departing from thence, we passed several large villages, where I was constantly taken for a Moor, and became the subject of much merriment to the Bambarrans, who, seeing me drive my horse before me, laughed heartily at my appearance. 'He has been at Mecca,' says one; 'you may see that by his clothes.' Another asked me if my horse was sick. A third wished to purchase it, etc., so that I believe the very slaves were ashamed to be seen in my company. Just before it was dark we took up our lodging for the night at a small village, where I procured some victuals for myself and some corn for my horse at the moderate price of a button; and was told that I should see the Niger (which the negroes call Jolibar, or the Great Water) early the next day.

The lions are here very numerous. The gates are shut a little after sunset, and nobody is allowed to go

* Park's 'Life and Travels.'

out. The thoughts of seeing the Niger in the morning and the troublesome buzzing of mosquitoes prevented me from shutting my eyes during the night, and I had saddled my horse and was in readiness before daylight ; but on account of the wild beasts we were obliged to wait until the people were stirring and the gates opened. This happened to be a market-day at Sego, and the roads were everywhere filled with people carrying different articles to sell. We passed four large villages, and at eight o'clock saw the smoke over Sego. As we approached the town, I was fortunate enough to overtake the fugitive Kaartans, to whose kindness I had been so much indebted in my journey through Bambarra. They readily agreed to introduce me to the King, and we rode together through some marshy ground, where, as I was anxiously looking around for the river, one of them called out ' *Geo affilli !*' (See the water !), and looking forwards, I saw with infinite pleasure the great object of my mission —the long-sought-for majestic Niger, glittering in the morning sun, as broad as the Thames at Westminster, and flowing slowly *to the eastward.* I hastened to the brink, and having drunk of the water, lifted up my fervent thanks in prayer to the Great Ruler of all things for having thus far crowned my endeavours with success.

The circumstances of the Niger's flowing towards the east, and its collateral points, did not, however, excite my surprise, for although I had left Europe in great hesitation on this subject, and rather believed that it ran in the contrary direction, I had made such frequent inquiries during my progress concerning this river, and received from negroes of different nations such clear and decisive assurances that its general course was *towards the rising sun,* as scarce left any doubt on my mind, and

more especially as I knew that Major Houghton had
collected similar information in the same manner.

Sego, the capital of Bambarra, at which I had now
arrived, consists, properly speaking, of four distinct towns
—two on the northern bank of the Niger, called Sego
Korro and Sego Boo; and two on the southern bank,
called Sego Soo Korro and Sego See Korro. They are
all surrounded with high mud walls. The houses are
built of clay, of a square form, with flat roofs; some of
them have two storeys, and many of them are white-
washed. Besides these buildings, Moorish mosques are
seen in every quarter, and the streets, though narrow,
are broad enough for every useful purpose in a country
where wheel carriages are entirely unknown. From the
best inquiries I could make, I have reason to believe that
Sego contains altogether about 30,000 inhabitants. The
King of Bambarra constantly resides at Sego See Korro.
He employs a great many slaves in conveying people
over the river, and the money they receive (though the fare
is only ten kowrie shells for each individual) furnishes a
considerable revenue to the King in the course of a year.

The canoes are of a singular construction, each of
them being formed of the trunks of two large trees
rendered concave and joined together, not side by side, but
endways, the junction being exactly across the middle of
the canoe. They are, therefore, very long and dispropor-
tionately narrow, and have neither decks nor masts;
they are, however, very roomy, for I observed in one
of them four horses and several people crossing over the
river. When we arrived at this ferry, with a view to
pass over to that part of the town in which the King
resides, we found a great number waiting for a passage.
They looked at me with silent wonder, and I distinguished with concern many Moors among them. There

were three different places of embarkation, and the ferry-
men were very diligent añd expeditious; but, from the
crowd of people, I could not immediately obtain a
passage, and sat down upon the bank of the river to wait
for a more favourable opportunity. The view of this
extensive city, the numerous canoes upon the river, the
crowded population, and the cultivated state of the surrounding country, formed altogether a prospect of civilization and magnificence which I little expected to find in
the bosom of Africa.

I waited more than two hours without having an
opportunity of crossing the river, during which time
the people who had crossed carried information to Man-
song, the King, that a white man was waiting for a
passage, and was coming to see him. He immediately
sent over one of his chief men, who informed me that the
King could not possibly see me until he knew what had
brought me into his country, and that I must not presume
to cross the river without the King's permission. He
therefore advised me to lodge at a distant village, to
which he pointed, for the night, and said that in the
morning he would give me further instructions how to
conduct myself. This was very discouraging. However,
as there was no remedy, I set off for the village, where
I found, to my great mortification, that no person would
admit me into his house. I was regarded with astonishment and fear, and was obliged to sit all day without
victuals in the shade of a tree ; and the night threatened
to be very uncomfortable, for the wind rose, and there
was great appearance of a heavy rain ; and the wild
beasts are so very numerous in the neighbourhood, that
I should have been under the necessity of climbing up
the tree and resting among the branches.

About sunset, however, as I was preparing to pass the

night in this manner, and had turned my horse loose, that he might graze at liberty, a woman, returning from the labours of the field, stopped to observe me; and perceiving that I was weary and dejected, inquired into my situation, which I briefly explained to her, whereupon, with looks of great compassion, she took up my saddle and bridle, and told me to follow her. Having conducted me into her hut, she lighted up a lamp, spread a mat on the floor, and told me that I might remain there for the night. Finding that I was very hungry, she said she would procure me something to eat. She accordingly went out, and returned in a short time with a very fine fish, which, having caused it to be half broiled upon some embers, she gave me for supper.

The rites of hospitality being thus performed towards a stranger in distress, my worthy benefactress (pointing to the mat, and telling me I might sleep there without apprehension) called to the female part of her family, who had stood gazing on me all the while in fixed astonishment, to resume their task of spinning cotton, in which they continued to employ themselves great part of the night. They lightened their labour by songs, one of which was composed extempore, for I was myself the subject of ·it. It was sung by one of the young women, the rest joining in a sort of chorus. The air was sweet and plaintive, and the words, literally translated, were these : ' The winds roared, and the rains fell. The poor white man, faint and weary, came and sat under our tree. He has no mother to bring him milk, no wife to grind his corn.' *Chorus :* ' Let us pity the white man ; no mother has he,' etc. Trifling as this recital may appear to the reader, to a person in my situation the circumstance was affecting in the highest degree. I was oppressed by such unexpected kindness, and sleep fled

from my eyes. In the morning I presented my com-
passionate landlady with two of the four brass buttons
which remained on my waistcoat, the only recompense I
could make her.

40. MUNGO PARK'S LAST LETTER TO LORD CAMDEN.*

WRITTEN FROM SANSANDIG, NOVEMBER, 1805.

I am sorry to say that of forty-four Europeans who
left the Gambia in perfect health, five only are at present
alive, namely, three soldiers (one deranged in his mind),
Lieutenant Martyn, and myself. From this account I
am afraid that your Lordship will be apt to consider
matters as in a very hopeless state; but I assure you I
am far from despairing. With the assistance of one of
the soldiers, I have changed a large canoe into a tolerably
good schooner, on board of which this day I have hoisted
the British flag, and shall set sail to the east, with the
fixed resolution to *discover the termination of the Niger, or
perish in the attempt.* I have heard nothing that I can
depend on respecting the remote course of this mighty
stream, but I am more and more inclined to think that it
can end nowhere but in the sea.

My dear friend Mr. Anderson, and likewise Mr. Scott,
are both dead; but though all the Europeans who are
with me should die, and though I were myself half dead,
I would still persevere; and if I could not succeed in the
object of my journey, I would at last *die on the Niger.*

* Park's ' Life and Travels.'

41. MUNGO PARK'S FATE.

COMMANDER CLAPPERTON,* 1826.

I was talking with a man that is married to one of my landlady's female slaves about the manners of the Cumbrie and about England, when he gave the following account of the death of Park and his companions, of which he was an eye-witness. He said that when the boat came down the river, it happened unfortunately just at the time that the Fellatas first rose in arms, and were ravaging Goober and Zamfra ; that the Sultan of Boussa, on hearing that the persons in the boat were white men, and that the boat was different from any that had ever been seen before, as she had a house at one end, called his people together from the neighbouring towns, attacked and killed them, not doubting that they were the advance guard of the Fellata army then ravaging Soudan under the command of Malem Danfodio, the father of the present Bello ; that one of the white men was a tall man with long hair ; that they fought for three days before they were all killed ; that the people in the neighbourhood were very much alarmed, and great numbers fled to Nyffé and other countries, thinking that the Fellatas were certainly coming among them. The number of persons in the boat was only four—two white men and two blacks ; that they found great treasure in the boat ; but that the people had all died who ate of the meat that was found in her. This account I believe to be the most correct of all that I have yet got, and was told without my putting any questions or showing any eagerness for him to go on with his story.

* ' Journal of a Second Expedition.' (Murray, 1829.)

42. THE BENIN RIVER (NOT THEN KNOWN TO BE A MOUTH OF THE NIGER).

BOSMAN,* 1700.

This river sprouts itself into innumerable branches, some of which are so wide that they very well deserve the name of rivers ; and the banks of each of them are inhabited by a particular nation, governed by its own king. The multitude of its branches renders the sailing up this river so difficult that a pilot is absolutely necessary. . . .

Its length and source I have not been able to discover, no Negro being able to give me an exact account of it ; but I believe its branches extend into all the circumjacent countries, for I have seen several men that came from Ardra, Calbary, and several other places in order to trade, which were taken on this river by the robbers and sold for slaves. These robbers, or pirates, live just at the mouth of the river, and are called the Pirates of Usa. They are very poor, and live only on robbery. They sail hence to all parts of this river, and seize all that lights in their way, whether men, beasts, or goods, all which they sell to the first that come hither for victuals, with which they are not at all provided. . . .

Several miles upwards from the mouth of the river the land is everywhere low and morassy, and its banks all along adorned with great numbers of high and low trees, and the country all about it divided into islands by the multiplicity of its branches ; besides which, here are several sorts of floating isles, or lands covered with reed, which are driven by the winds, or Travadoes, from one place to another, by which means they often happen in

* Pinkerton's ' Voyages,' 1814.

our way, and oblige us to steer a different course, on which occasions pilots or guides are very convenient.

The river itself is very pleasant, but very unwholesome, as most of the rivers on the coast seem to be naturally, which I am apt to think is occasioned by the continual contagious exhalations which hover about them, more especially those in low ground and morasses. To which may be added another, and not less plague—the innumerable millions of gnats, which the Portuguese call musquitoes, for the land, as I have already told you, being very woody, is insupportably pestered with these vermin, especially in the nights, when they attack us in whole legions, and sting so severely, that several persons have been so marked with pustules that it was impossible to know them. This torment, which deprives us of our natural rest, heightened by the unwholesomeness of the climate, continually occasions a great mortality amongst our men. You very well know that this is my second voyage to this river, and that the first time I was here we lost half our men, and at present the number of our dead on board is not less, and the remainder are most of them sick, which strikes such a general terror into the sailors that the boldest of them is afraid of his life.

Five of our sailors were so rashly impious as to throw dice who should die or live to come out of this river. They over-persuaded my eldest servant to throw for his chance with them, and the highest cast being esteemed safest, he threw eleven. And it is really remarkable that this lad is yet alive, but the other five died all in the river of Benin.

Bating the said contagion of the climate, this is a very desirable place of trade, by reason of the pleasantness of the river and adjacent country, which is very even ground, without hills, and yet rises by gentle degrees,

which affords the most agreeable prospect in the world,
which is yet improved by the multitude of trees which
stand so regular, as if they were designedly planted in
that order.

43. DOWN THE NIGER.

R. AND J. LANDER,* 1830.

We looked around us for a landing-place, where we
might rest awhile, but we could find none, for every
village which we saw after that hour was unfortunately
situated behind large thick morasses and sloughy bogs,
through which, after various tedious and provoking trials,
we found it impossible to penetrate. We were employed
three hours in the afternoon in endeavouring to find a
landing at some village, and though we saw them distinctly enough from the water, we could not find a
passage through the morasses, behind which they lay.
Therefore we were compelled to relinquish the attempt
and continue our course on the Niger. We passed
several beautiful islands in the course of the day, all
cultivated and inhabited, but low and flat. The width
of the river appeared to vary considerably; sometimes it
seemed to be two or three miles across, and at others
double that width. The current drifted us along very
rapidly, and we guessed it to be running at the rate of
three or four miles an hour. The direction of the stream
continued nearly east.

The day had been excessively warm, and the sun set
in beauty and grandeur, shooting forth rays, tinged with
the most radiant hues, which extended to the zenith.
Nevertheless, the appearance of the firmament, all

* 'Expedition to Explore the Course of the Niger.' (Murray,
1833.)

glorious as it was, betokened a coming storm; the wind whistled wildly through the tall rushes, and darkness soon covered the earth like a veil. This rendered us more anxious than ever to land somewhere, we cared not where, and to endeavour to procure shelter for the night, if not in a village, at least under a tree. Accordingly, rallying the drooping spirits of our men, we encouraged them to renew their exertions by setting them the example, and our canoe darted silently and swiftly down the current. We were enabled to steer her rightly by the vividness of the lightning, which flashed across the water continually, and by this means also we could distinguish any danger before us, and avoid the numerous small islands with which the river is interspersed, and which otherwise might have embarrassed us very seriously. But though we could perceive almost close to us several lamps burning in comfortable-looking huts, and could plainly distinguish the voices of their occupants, and though we exerted all our strength to get at them, we were foiled in every attempt, by reason of the sloughs and fens, and we were at last obliged to abandon them in despair.

Some of these lights, after leading us a long way, eluded our search, and vanished from our sight like an *ignis fatuus*, and others danced about, we knew not how nor where. But what was more vexatious than all, after we had got into an inlet, and toiled and tugged for a full half-hour against the current, which in this little channel was uncommonly rapid, to approach a village from which we thought it flowed, both village and lights seemed to sink into the earth, the sound of the people's voices ceased of a sudden, and when we fancied we were actually close to the spot, we strained our eyes in vain to see a single hut—all was gloomy, dismal, cheerless, and solitary. It seemed the work of enchantment; everything was as visionary as 'sceptres grasped in sleep.'

We had paddled along the banks a distance of not less than thirty miles, every inch of which we had attentively examined, but not a bit of dry land could anywhere be discovered which was firm enough to bear our weight. Therefore we resigned ourselves to circumstances, and all of us having been refreshed with a little cold rice and honey, and water from the stream, we permitted the canoe to drift down with the current, for our men were too much fatigued with the labours of the day to work any longer.

But here a fresh evil arose which we were unprepared to meet. An incredible number of hippopotami arose very near us, and came plashing, snorting, and plunging all round the canoe, and placed us in imminent danger. Thinking to frighten them off, we fired a shot or two at them, but the noise only called up from the water, and out of the fens, about as many more of their unwieldy companions, and we were more closely beset than before. Our people, who had never in all their lives been exposed in a canoe to such huge and formidable beasts, trembled with fear and apprehension, and absolutely wept aloud; and their terror was not a little increased by the dreadful peals of thunder which rattled over their heads, and by the awful darkness which prevailed, broken at intervals by flashes of lightning, whose powerful glare was truly awful.

Our people tell us that these formidable animals frequently upset canoes in the river, when everyone in them is sure to perish. These came so close to us, that we could reach them with the butt-end of a gun. When I fired at the first, which I must have hit, everyone of them came to the surface of the water, and pursued us

9—2

so fast over to the north bank, that it was with the
greatest difficulty imaginable we could keep before them.
Having fired a second time, the report of my gun was
followed by a loud roaring noise, and we seemed to
increase our distance from them.   There were two
Bornou men among our crew who were not so frightened
as the rest, having seen some of these creatures before on
Lake Tchad, where, they say, plenty of them abound . . . .

We observed a bank on the north side of the river
shortly after this, and I proposed halting on it for the
night, for I wished much to put my foot on firm land
again.   This, however, not one of the crew would consent
to, saying, that if the *Gewow Roua*, or water-elephant, did
not kill them, the crocodiles certainly would do so before
the morning. . . .

Our canoe is only large enough to hold us all when
sitting, so that we have no chance of lying down.   Had
we been able to muster up 30,000 cowries at Rabba, we
might have purchased one which would have carried us
all very comfortably.   A canoe of this sort would have
served us for living in entirely; we should have had no
occasion to land, excepting to obtain our provisions, and
having performed our day's journey might have anchored
fearlessly at night.

Finding we could not induce our people to land, we
agreed to continue on all night.   The eastern horizon
became very dark, and the lightning more and more
vivid; indeed, we never recollect having seen such
strong forked lightning before in our lives.   All this
denoted the approach of a storm.   At 11 p.m. it blew
somewhat stronger than a gale, and at midnight the
storm was at its height.   The wind was so furious that
it swept the water over the sides of the canoe several
times, so that she was in danger of filling.   Driven

about by the wind, our frail little bark became un-
manageable; but at length we got near a bank, which
in some measure protected us, and we were fortunate
enough to lay hold of a thorny tree, against which we
were driven, and which was growing nearly in the centre
of the stream. Presently we fastened the canoe to its
branches, and wrapping our cloaks round our persons,
for we felt overpowered with fatigue, and with our legs
dangling half over the sides of the little vessel into the
water, which for want of room we were compelled to do,
we lay down to sleep.

There is something, I believe, in the nature of a
tempest which is favourable to slumber—at least, so
thought my brother—for though the thunder continued
to roar, and the wind to rage, though the rain beat in
our faces, and our .canoe lay rocking like a cradle, still
he slept soundly. The wind kept blowing hard from the
eastward till after midnight, when it became calm. The
rain then descended in torrents, accompanied with thunder
and lightning of the most awful description. We lay in
our canoe, drenched with rain, and our little vessel was
filling so fast, that two people were obliged to be constantly baling out the water to keep her afloat. The
water-elephants, as the natives term the hippopotami,
frequently came snorting near us, but fortunately did
not touch our canoe.

44. THE MOUTH OF THE NIGER.

R. AND J. LANDER,* 1830.

At half-past eight in the evening, to our great satisfaction, we found ourselves influenced by the tide. We

* 'Expedition to Explore the Course of the Niger.' (Murray,
1833.)

had previously observed an appearance of foam on the
water, which might have been carried up by the flood-
tide from the mouth of the river ; but we now felt certain
of being within its influence. We were constantly an-
noyed by the canoe running aground on a bank or sticking
fast in the underwood, which delayed our progress considerably, and the men were obliged to get out to lighten
and lift the canoe off them. Our track was through a
narrow creek arched over by mangroves, so as to form a
complete avenue, which in many places was so thick as
to be totally impenetrable by the light above. At 10 p.m.
a heavy shower of rain wetted us thoroughly, and after
this was over, the dripping from the trees which overhung the canoe kept us in constant rain nearly all night.
The smell from decayed vegetable substances was sickly
and exceedingly disagreeable.

Monday, November 15*th.*—Through these gloomy and
dismal passages we travelled during the whole of last
night without stopping, unless for a few minutes at a
time, to disengage ourselves from the pendent shoots of
the mangrove and spreading brambles in which we occasionally became entangled. These luxuriant natives of
the soil are so intricately woven, that it would be next
to impossible to eradicate them. Their roots and branches
are the receptacles of ooze, mud, and filth of all kinds,
exhaling a peculiarly offensive odour, which, no doubt,
possesses highly deleterious qualities.

      *   *   *   *   *

Of all the wretched, filthy, and contemptible places in
this world of ours, none can present to the eye of a
stranger so miserable an appearance or can offer such
disgusting and loathsome sights as this abominable
Brass town. Dogs, goats, and other animals run about
the dirty streets half starved, whose hungry looks can

only be exceeded by the famishing appearance of the men, women, and children, which bespeaks the penury and wretchedness to which they are reduced; whilst the persons of many of them are covered with odious boils, and their huts are falling to the ground from neglect and decay.

Brass, properly speaking, consists of two towns of nearly equal size, containing about a thousand inhabitants each, and built on the borders of a kind of basin, which is formed by a number of rivulets entering it from the Niger through forests of mangrove bushes. One of them is under the domination of a noted scoundrel called *King Jacket*, who has already been spoken of; and the other is governed by a rival chief, named *King Forday*. These towns are situated directly opposite each other and within the distance of eighty yards, and are built on a marshy ground, which occasions the huts to be always wet.

Another place, called 'Pilot's town' by Europeans, from the number of pilots that reside in it, is situated nearly at the mouth of the First Brass River (which we understand is the '*Nun*' River of Europeans), and at the distance of sixty or seventy miles from hence. This town acknowledges the authority of both kings, having been originally peopled by settlers from each of their towns. At the ebb of the tide the basin is left perfectly dry with the exception of small gutters, and presents a smooth and almost unvaried surface of black mud, which emits an intolerable odour, owing to the decomposition of vegetable substances and the quantity of filth and nastiness which is thrown into the basin by the inhabitants of both towns. Notwithstanding this nuisance, both children and grown-up persons may be seen sporting in the mud whenever the tide goes out, all naked,

and amusing themselves in the same manner as if they
were on shore.

The Brass people grow neither yams nor bananas, nor
grain of any kind, cultivating only the plantain as an
article of food, which, with the addition of a little fish,
forms their principal article of diet. Yams, however, are
freely imported from Eboe and other countries by the
chief people, who re-sell great quantities of them to the
shipping that may happen to be in the river. They are
enabled to do this by the very considerable profits which
accrue to them from their trading transactions with
people residing further inland, and from the palm oil
which they themselves manufacture, and which they
dispose of to the Liverpool traders.

The soil in the vicinity of Brass is for the most part
poor and marshy, though it is covered with a rank,
luxuriant, and impenetrable vegetation. Even in the
hands of an active, industrious race it would offer almost
insuperable obstacles to general cultivation, but with its
present possessors the mangrove itself can never be
extirpated, and the country will, it is likely enough,
maintain its present appearance till the end of time.

  *   *   *   *   *

Our canoe passed through the narrow creeks, sometimes winding under avenues of mangrove-trees, and at
others expanding into small lakes occasioned by the
overflowing of the river. The captain of the canoe, a
tall sturdy fellow, was standing up directing its course,
occasionally hallooing as we came to a turn in the creek
to the fetish, and where an echo was returned half a
glass of rum and a piece of yam and fish were thrown
into the water. I had never seen this done before, and
on asking Boy the reason why he was throwing away the
provisions thus, he asked : ' Did you not hear the fetish ?'

The captain of the canoe replied : ' Yes.' ' That is for
the fetish,' said Boy. ' If we do not feed him and do
good for him, he will kill us or make us poor and sick.'
I could not help smiling at the ignorance of the poor
creatures, but such is their firm belief.

We had pursued our course in this manner, which had
been principally to the west, till about three in the afternoon, when we came to a branch of the river about two
hundred yards wide, and seeing a small village a short
distance before us, we stopped there for the purpose
of obtaining some dried fish. Having supplied our
wants and proceeded on, about an hour afterwards we
again stopped, that our people might eat something.
Boy very kindly presented me with a large piece of yam,
reserving to himself all the fish we had got at the village,
and after making a hearty meal off them, he fell asleep.
While he was snoring by my side the remainder of the
fish attracted my notice, and not feeling half satisfied
with the yam he had given me, I felt an irresistible
inclination to taste them. Conscience acquitted me on
the score of hunger, and hinted that such an opportunity
should not be lost, and accordingly I very quickly de-
molished two small ones. Although entirely raw, they
were delicious, and I do not remember to have enjoyed
anything with a better relish in all my life.

There is scarcely a spot of dry land to be seen anywhere ; all is covered with water and mangrove-trees.
After remaining about half an hour here, we again went
forward, and at seven in the evening arrived in the
Second Brass River, which is a large branch of the
Quorra. We kept our course down it about due south,
and half an hour afterwards I heard the welcome sound
of the surf on the beach.

45. THE NIGER TO-DAY.

LIEUTENANT S. VANDELEUR,* 1897.

In place of the long interminable stretch of sand, topped
by the dark green line of trees and bushes, which forms
the west coast of Africa, the eye now rested on a multitude
of creeks or rivers, intersecting interminable mangrove
swamps, and merging themselves in the thin mist overhanging the horizon ; and one could not wonder that the
mouth and outlet of the great River Niger was unknown
for so many centuries, and that almost as much mystery
was attached to it as to the source of the Nile.

Times have altered since then. Now large steamers
and speedy launches ply to and fro for hundreds of miles
up the river, though in the dry season—lasting eight
months—vessels exceeding four feet draught can navigate
only a short distance. It was difficult at first to see how
we could keep in the right channel, as in the launch we
passed countless islands of mangroves, and every turn
appeared just the same as another. To a newcomer the
latter would seem to be nice green woods ; but on closer
inspection they prove to be nothing but thousands of
white roots growing out of the slimy, yellow sand, in
which they find a treacherous foothold, and above them,
interlaced together, stretch the branches and green foliage
which have given rise to the deception.

In an hour or two we come to the first station of the
Royal Niger Company, called Burutu, where a small
piece of *terra-firma* has been utilized in this submerged
region ; and there are several warehouses, also a house

* 'Campaigning on the Upper Nile and Niger.' (Methuen,
1898.)

in course of construction for the official in charge. As we proceed, the banks become more defined and harder, and on rounding a corner we come to the first signs of the natives. A few small square houses or huts, made of wattle and mud, with roofs of dried palm-leaves and reeds, lie clustered together, the inhabitants of which maintain themselves by the fish they catch. Farther on the scenery alters entirely. The mangrove swamps have given place to high banks, covered with long green grass and fine trees. Large villages are thronged with natives of rather an ugly and repulsive type, most of them wearing coloured cloths round their loins. Formerly they were undoubted cannibals, and accustomed to kill and eat their captives taken in war; and it is rumoured that even now a morsel of human flesh is not despised when obtainable, and I am told the human foot is a great delicacy. Behind and on each side of the village are banana groves, with their long, broad, shady leaves; and over all rise the lofty, thin palm-trees, the feathery leaves of which taper gradually to the end, and droop gracefully over. Sometimes pretty acacia trees, and cotton trees with coloured blossoms, meet the eye.

Some of the women are painted with cross lines of blue or red, and in a few instances they have brass-wire bangles, or are covered with a slate-coloured chalk—a strange mode of adornment. Fishing-nets and baskets lie scattered about on the bank, and a number of dug-out canoes are fastened to the side. Here is one in course of construction. A man is shaping it out with an adze, after which the inside will be further burnt away by means of fire. Some of these canoes are really almost miniature ones, and so small are they that their sides appear nearly level with the water's edge. About 12 inches in width, they must be hard to balance, yet natives can be seen gliding along in them under the banks at a great pace.

To anyone of an adventurous turn of mind there is something very taking in thus rapidly steaming up a great waterway into the heart of Central Africa. At every turn, new sights and strange beings meet the eye, and one wonders what there can be behind the apparently trackless bush and jungle which line the banks, except where the human hand has made a clearing for habitation. On the sandbanks, which are now exposed in this the dry season, lie enormous crocodiles, which waddle off into the water with a splash at our approach; and on the second day, hippopotami can be seen poking their big goggle-eyed heads out of the water at a safe distance from us. This day we reached in the early morning a station called Asaye. It was near here that Lieutenant Mizon, after making his way up the river in a steam-launch, unknown to the Company's officials, was surprised by the natives at night, and severely wounded, some of his men being killed. The nights are dark, and we have to anchor until morning; even now the Maxim gun is loaded, and a watch is kept to guard against surprise. Though there has been such success in doing away with strife and bringing peace to these regions, it is still just as well to be ready for emergencies. In old days villages used to raid one another, and native traders plied up and down the river in their canoes at the risk of their lives.

The farther one ascends up the river the more it improves. Stations are passed where palm oil and the valuable rubber are collected in readiness for transport to England. Not until the third day do we arrive at Asaba, the administrative headquarters—a pretty place, situated about 40 feet above the river, which is here just over a mile broad. The grounds are well laid out, and mango-trees, baobab-trees, and feather palms line the walks.

Farther on, the country becomes drier and burnt-up-looking. Great sandy islands obstruct the channel of the river, and the course is more difficult to find. Twice we ran aground, and were delayed for three hours, having to pull ourselves off by means of a wire cable. The scenery on approaching Lokoja is very fine, high hills, some cone-shaped, rising up on each side. And here, on the fifth day, we reached our destination, the base of the forthcoming expedition.

Lokoja presented a very busy appearance, and the bank of the river was crowded with fatigue-parties of soldiers and natives, engaged loading the stern-wheelers and launches for the forthcoming expedition. After the naked savages we had seen along the banks of the Lower Niger, it was a change indeed to see the natives here all covered with cloth, tobes, and enormous turbans.

46. THE SOURCE OF THE NIGER.

COLONEL J. K. TROTTER, 1896.*

Our guide now told us that the valley in front of us was that of the Tembi, the longest tributary of the Niger, and we knew then that we were standing upon the boundary-line between British and French territory, the watershed dividing the streams flowing into the Niger from those running westwards into Sierra Leone. Of the valley in front of us little could be seen. The country was clothed with the cane-brake, which grows to 10 feet high, and which is such a complete obstacle both to movement and to observation. Still, we could

* 'The Niger Sources.' (Methuen and Co., 1898.)

discern the green foliage which indicated that a water-course was there.

Our guides pointed out to us the valley, but neither threats nor persuasion would induce them to lead us to the head. Any attempt to force them would only have ended in their lying to us, leading us astray, and escaping at the first opportunity. As a matter of fact, they both disappeared before we reached the valley. In such a country nothing is easier than to slip aside into the bush when out of observation for a moment and to disappear beyond all danger of pursuit. The natives of this country have the greatest dread of the Niger source. They regard it as the seat of the devil, who is the only supreme being they worship; and they believe that to look upon it is to meet certain death within the year. Our visit to the place was regarded as very likely to provoke the evil one into an undesirable form of activity in the neighbourhood, and in order to prevent this, the inhabitants of the nearest village sacrificed, some days later, a white fowl, and sprinkled its blood on the trees near the upper slope of the Tembi Valley.

Deserted by our guides, we forced our way through the cane-brake which covered the slope of the ridge. We were now in the Tembi basin, but the actual valley in which the stream ran lay still some way in front of us. At length we reached the green foliage, and, having done so, turned immediately southward, and followed the valley till we turned its head. We knew then that we were close to the object of our search. Accompanied by Captain Cayrade of the French Commission, we struck into the valley on the eastern side and cut our way down to the bottom. This valley, like almost every water-course in that part of this country, consists of a deep ravine, with steeply sloping sides covered with trees,

creepers, and bush, and very difficult to penetrate.
Cutting our way through the undergrowth, we crept and
clambered down the slippery slopes till we reached the
bottom, and came to a moss-covered rock, from which
a tiny spring issues, and has made a pool below. The
foliage at this spot is green, most luxuriant, and beautiful ; and as one looks on the birthplace of the Niger, it is
easy to imagine one's self at a dripping well in some wood
in England. The spot is shady—too shady indeed, for
sun, light, and air are in one case altogether, and in the
other too much, excluded. The darkness is characteristic of the valleys of this land. The foliage is so dense,
and the creepers are so abundant, that the sun cannot
penetrate them ; and it is probably owing to this, and
to the immense quantity of decaying vegetation, that
malaria is to be found even in the higher regions of the
interior.

In the pool which receives the first waters of the Niger
we found a bottle with a note inserted, announcing that
Captain Brouet, a French officer, had visited the place in
1895, and on the rock his initials, G. B., were cut. That
the bottle was allowed to remain untouched is a proof
that no native approaches the place, for in this country a
bottle is a highly-valued article of trade. A few days
later we found some natives with fruit, of which there is
very little in this particular neighbourhood, and we
brought out all our trade goods to offer them a selection
in exchange for their bananas and papaws. After
examining everything carefully, and after looking with
longing eyes on our cottons and our beads, they eventually fixed their affections on an empty pint champagne
bottle, and for this they gave us all the fruit they had.
Our personal attendants and hammock-boys made no
small profit out of the local demand for empty bottles,

which were their perquisites, and which they quickly
converted into rice, cassava, fowls, or native tobacco.

The natives, amongst their other superstitions, have a
great dread of drinking the water of the Niger. Not
having any superstitions, we drank it freely when we
visited the source, and not long afterwards were fain
to admit that the natives were wiser than we. Indeed,
judging from its effects, there is some ground for
believing that the river is indeed haunted.

PART V.

SOUTH AND SOUTH-CENTRAL AFRICA.

INTRODUCTION.

THE South Africa with which men concern themselves
to-day is a large region, extending, indeed, from the
Cape of Good Hope to the great river Zambesi. The
newspapers day by day sufficiently inform us what it is.
The following extracts are therefore designed rather to
remind us what it was, and that not so very long ago.
That the Dutch were the first white colonists of this
country would be plain, even if their descendants were
not still living there, and still spreading over fresh regions
which, when the English arrived, were still unoccupied.
For not only do the names of plants and animals, towns
and districts, remain to tell what nation conferred them,
but so thoroughly has the Dutch language adapted itself
to the features of the country, that the English traveller
finds himself obliged as he travels to call the grassy plain
the 'veldt,' a ravine a 'kloof,' a waterhole a 'vley.'

But among the people who were there before the
Dutch there were some of whom few are now left, and
who will leave few traces behind them. The black races
of Africa remain and multiply under the white man's
rule; but the black races were by no means the only
occupants of the southern end of Africa, where the yellow
Hottentots held their ground, and where also—especially

in the desert regions—there still survived the dwarf race
of Bushmen, now fast vanishing from the earth.   In the
science of the chase these little hunters far excelled the
higher races who despised them, and, feeble and defenceless as they seemed to their fellow-men, were able to
hold their own amid hosts of the largest and fiercest wild
animals that any part of the world has been able to show.
For the plains of South Africa swarmed with life in
almost incredible abundance: elephants, rhinoceroses
and giraffes, lions, hyenas and jackals, and, above all,
antelopes of many kinds, and sometimes in countless
herds, held undisputed sway over all the regions that are
now white men's farms or white men's mining towns, as
well as in those remoter tracts which are only beginning
to be disturbed by the feet of European immigrants
searching for gold.

This search has made us acquainted with a strange
discovery, that the gold mines in the wilds of remote
Mashonaland have been worked already, and worked by
people who have left behind them the ruined remains of
great buildings such as no South African race of to-day
could even form the conception of erecting.   It is only
within the last few years that any close examination of
these ruins has been made, but it will be seen (see 54 and
55) that their existence was reported to the early Portuguese, and that the very name of Zimbabwe reached the
ears of the Dutch two hundred years and more ago.
The theory of the Portuguese, that this mysterious
country was the Biblical Ophir from which King
Solomon three thousand years ago obtained his gold,
does not lack defenders at this day.

The Victoria Falls of the Zambesi were discovered and
thus named by Livingstone in 1855.   Their old native
name is said to have meant that smoke there makes a

sound, the spray being seen at a great distance rising like clouds of smoke. They are probably to be considered the greatest waterfall in the world.

---

47. THE ORIGIN OF CAPE COLONY.

J. A. FROUDE.*

The Cape Colony, as we ought to know, but in practice we always forget, was originally a Dutch colony. Two centuries ago, when the Hollanders were the second maritime power in the world—perhaps not even second —they occupied and settled the southern extremity of Africa. They easily conquered the Hottentots and Bushmen, acting as we ourselves also acted invariably in similar circumstances. They cleared out the wild beasts, built towns, laid out roads, enclosed and ploughed the land, planted forests and vineyards.

Better colonists or more successful did not exist than the Dutch. They throve and prospered, and continued to thrive and prosper till the close of the last century. If we compare the success of the Dutch in the management of uncivilized tribes with our own, in all parts of the world, it will be found that, although their rule is stricter than ours, and to appearance harsher, they have had fewer native wars than we have had. There has been less violence and bloodshed, and the natives living under them have not been less happy or less industrious.

Holland in the Revolutionary war was seized by the French Directory. The English, at the request of the Prince of Orange, took the Cape under their protection. It was on the high road to India ; there was then no alternative route by the Suez Canal ; and so important a

* 'Oceana.' (Longmans, 1886.)

station could not be permitted to fall into the hands of
Napoleon. At the peace of Amiens it was restored to
Holland, and the English garrison was withdrawn. On
the war breaking out again, our occupation was renewed ;
a fleet was sent out, with a strong invading force. The
Cape Dutch resisted—fought a gallant action, in which
they were largely helped by native allies ; they yielded
only in the belief that, as before, the occupation would
be temporary, and that their country would be finally
given back to them when the struggle was over. It was
not given back.

48. A DESCRIPTION OF THE BOERS.

A. SPARRMAN,* 1785.

About ten o'clock I took shelter from the rain in a
farm-house, where I found the female slaves singing
psalms while they were at their needlework. Their
master, being possessed with a zeal for religion quite
unusual in this country, had prevailed with them to
adopt this godly custom ; but with that spirit of economy
which universally prevails among these colonists, he had
not permitted them to be initiated into the community of
Christians by baptism, since by that means, according to
the laws of the land, they would have obtained their
freedom, and he would have lost them from his service.

This very godly *boor* was born at Berlin, and had been
mate of a ship in the East Indies. This occasioned us
to enter into a conversation on the victories of his much-
loved monarch, and in the space of an hour after that,
upon every subject that could be imagined. My throat
still felt as if it was burnt up with pepper, and my

* 'Voyage to the Cape.' (Robinson, 1785.)

stomach was tormented with hunger. The former was assuaged by a couple of glasses of wine, but being ashamed to complain of the latter, I left it to its fate to wait till noon (when, perhaps, I might chance to get an invitation from some good soul), and returned to my botanical calling and occupation among the shrubs and bushes, with which this country is almost entirely covered, excepting such spots as are cultivated.

Hardly a stick of wood, indeed scarcely any wild tree, is to be seen here. The soil hereabouts, viz., round about *Tyger-berg* and *Koe-berg*, is, to all appearance, mostly a dry barren sand or gravel; yet in this district, so full of hillocks, there are certain dales covered with mould, and yielding a plentiful harvest to a few peasants, who apply to the culture of lemon, orange, and pomegranate-trees. At three in the afternoon I arrived at the house of farmer *Van der Spoei*, who was a widower, and an African born. . . . Without seeming to take the least notice, he stood stock still in the house-passage, waiting for my coming up, and then did not stir a single step to meet me, but taking me by the hand greeted me with *Good-day! Welcome! How are you? Who are you? A glass of wine? A pipe of tobacco? Will you eat anything?* I answered his questions in the same order as he put them, and at the same time accepted of the offer he made at the close of them. His daughter, a clever, well-behaved girl, about twelve or fourteen years of age, set on the table a fine breast of lamb, with stewed carrots for sauce, and after dinner offered me tea with so good a grace that I hardly knew which to prefer, my entertainment or my fair attendant. Discretion and goodness of heart might be plainly read in the countenance and demeanour of both father and child. I several times addressed myself to my host in order to break in upon his silence. His answers were short and discreet; but upon the whole he never began the conversation himself any further than to ask me to stay with them that night; however, I took leave of him, not without being much affected with a benevolence as uncommon to be met with, as undeserved on my part. In my great zeal for botany, I did not pay the least attention to my stiff and wearied legs, but hobbled as well as I could over the dry and torrid hills, moving all the day long as if I was upon stilts.

49. CAPE COLONY EIGHTY YEARS AGO.

COWPER ROSE.*

I who had walked full twenty-four miles over the roughest ground, with a gun that weighed twenty pounds, found it impossible to keep up with my more active companions, and, seating myself on the ground, told the hunter to go and leave me, and on reaching the bivouac, to send my Hottentot and horse. ' It is impossible,' he replied; 'it will be a dark night; and even in the day, no one will find you here.' ' It is of no consequence; I do not wish to spoil your sport, but I can go no farther;' and I stretched myself on the ground, indifferent to the result. ' Were a rhinoceros to come down, I think you would find your legs.' ' No; nothing could make me mount that hill.' There was a consultation which I scarcely heard, and it was resolved that the little boy should remain with me; and that when I had rested, we should ascend the hill, lighting fires as we went, to mark our course.

The remainder of the party followed the elephants.

* ' Four Years in South Africa,' 1829.

In half an hour I again took my gun, which had been changed for one that would scarcely fire, and began to ascend the hill by an elephant path; the valley we had just left, and the side of the hill, were thickly covered with high dark bush, on my right so close as to prevent our seeing any object in that direction. We were slowly rising the ascent, when I heard the heavy gallop of a large animal approaching; my little companion was at some distance from me, blowing a lighted stick. 'Listen!' I said; the boy's eyes looked wild, and he fled from the sound, while I ran up the hill, not doubting that it was a rhinoceros; the heavy tramp was close to me, and I scarcely saw a large dark animal burst through the bush within a few yards of me, in the spot I had just quitted, and in the very path I was following. I did not stop, for, from the glimpse I caught, I believed it to be a rhinoceros. My young companion fired the bush, which I heard crackling, and in a few minutes came up to me. 'What a narrow escape!' he said. 'What was it—the rhinoceros?' 'Did you not see it close to you? It turned from the lighted bush.'

It was certainly a situation of danger, for the boldest hunter dreads and shuns this savage animal, and troops of lions have been known to fly before him; yet, without affecting any particular courage, I trusted rather to my heels than to my gun, which, as the event turned out, was fortunate, for when I attempted afterwards to fire, it snapped three times. I do not remember that I felt much fear, nor do I believe that, under similar circumstances, fear is natural—there is no time for it; every energy is employed in escape. In a gale at sea, on board a small coasting-brig, amidst the wild winds and waves of the Cape, though there was probably not one-twentieth part of the real danger, I have felt much

more, for there I was a useless being, and no exertions
of my own could avail, and memory and thought had
time to be busy.

We at length gained the summit of the hill, and saw
the elephants traversing the one before us, their huge
backs showing high above the bush ; we heard our companions fire, and saw the animals rush away, and one
charging towards us. We fired the bush and grass
around us, and stood in a circle of flame ; we listened,
but could hear nothing, and proceeded, lighting the bush
as we passed, and tracing the route of the elephant, and
the point at which he had been checked by the fire.
The effect of the shots, we afterwards heard, was the
death of a large female elephant that fell with ten balls
in her, each ball a death ; but she stood heaving her
back in agony, while her young calf went round and
moved under her, covered with the blood of its mother.
'Tis savage work ! We found on our route a small pond,
or rather puddle, but never was anything more welcome ;
and yet when I think of it, the thirst must have been
indeed extreme that would stoop to drink it ; the water
had been trodden into mud by the elephants, and we
were forced to suck it almost through closed teeth. It
was the vilest abomination that ever went down my
throat, and yet it refreshed me. We continued our
course, my young attendant trusting much to the
hunter's promise that he would watch the line of our
fires and join us ; but I had less faith in it, for we were
now far distant from each other, and the sun was fast
sinking, and the surrounding mountains assuming a
darker and darker hue. My little companion lighted the
bush and dry grass around, and fired repeatedly to tell
where we were ; but there was no answering shot.

The sun sank, but our fires only blazed the brighter

It was, in truth, a sight of no common beauty to see the
fire catch the dry green moss that hangs on the withered
branches and envelop the bush in wreaths of light and
fantastic flame, while the volumes of smoke, calmly
floating on the clear sky, assumed the rich hues of fire.
Dark night came on, and with it heavy dew that prevented the bush and grass from igniting; and the young
boy's spirit that had been so high during the day fell
amidst the surrounding gloom, and he still fired and
hallooed with the faint hope of having his halloo
returned; and he began to speak of being destroyed by
the surrounding elephants. I tried to laugh him out of
his fears. We collected dried wood for our night-fire,
and agreed to watch and sleep until daybreak. I took
the first five hours' watch, and was pleased to hear, from
the deep, regular breathing of my young companion, that
sleep and fatigue had overcome his terrors.

There was no moon, but the stars shone in brightness
and in beauty on a dark-blue sky. I listened, and at
times caught wild, remote sounds—the nameless sounds
of night. Who that has passed a night in savage solitudes has not felt how distinct its sounds are from those
of the day—has not discovered a voice and a language in
the night-wind as it moaned by, different from the rush
of any wind on which the sun ever shone, like spirit-
warnings from the past? I listened, and could imagine
in the distant booming, hollow noises, that hundreds of
elephants were crossing the hills, and again all was still
as death; and then would come the wild, melancholy
howl of the wolf, and its short whoop, the next nearer
than the first; and then, by sending a brighter flame
from the fire, all again would be hushed; and then the
stillness was interrupted by the croak of the night-raven,
as it sailed down the ravine, catching the scent of the

dead elephant. That ceased, and I heaped more dry wood upon the fire, until it threw up its bright flame, gleaming with an indistinct and lurid light on the surrounding bushes. Then came a strange noise as of some animal that was approaching us; it came nearer, and roused my little companion, who said it was the hyena, with its hideous laugh and chatter—the most wild, unnatural sound that breaks the silence of night in those tremendous solitudes. The morning star rose over the dark brow of the mountain; the first signs of day followed.

50. TRAVELLING BY OX-WAGGON.

A. SPARRMAN,* 1785.

There is not a bridge to be found in all Africa. We were therefore obliged to wade over some pretty deep brooks and rivers, so that herborizing, it must be owned, is a very troublesome business here; but then, on the other hand, the harvest is rich. As soon as I had sat myself down, I made a curious discovery of a remarkably prickly *rumex* (or dock), and likewise of the *tribulus terrestris.* Now and then we rambled up and down, recruiting for my regiment of insects and my collection of plants—an employment which, in proportion as it enlivened my mind, infused fresh spirits into my body, and strength into my limbs. These latter I had likewise an opportunity of resting on the following occasion. Among the waggons that overtook us, there was one drawn by six pair of oxen, after the fashion of the country. In this a slave lay asleep as drunk as David's sow, likewise in a great measure after the country fashion. Another, how-

* 'Voyage to the Cape,' 1785.

ever, more sober than he, sat at the helm with a whip,
the handle of which was three times the length of a man,
and the thong in proportion.   In this country they never
use reins to their oxen, for which reason, though he
flourished his whip about from right to left with great
dexterity, the beasts, not being under much discipline,
heaved continually from larboard to starboard, sometimes across the road, and sometimes alongside of it, so
that the driver was not unfrequently obliged to jump off
from the waggon in order to impress his sentiments with
the greater energy on the foremost oxen of the team.
The waggons are so large and wide in the carriage that
they cannot easily overturn, and where the road is worse
than ordinary, the foremost oxen are usually led.   Up in
the waggon sat a Dutchman, who being much hurt at
seeing me on foot, very courteously obliged me, together
with my servant, to get into the waggon and ride.   In
about the same latitude we were overtaken by a farmer.
We hailed one another, that is, we called to, and saluted
each other, as ships do at sea, and were informed by him
that he was a *Mother-country* lad (so the Europeans are
called here), and had a wife and family near the *twenty-
four rivers* at the distance of forty *uurs* from thence, in one
of the prettiest spots, to his mind, in the whole country.
But I now began to reflect that neither *Tournefort* in the
Levant, nor *Linnæus* in the *Lapland* mountains, nor any
other botanist, had ever gone out a herborizing in a six-
yoked waggon, and at the same time that my studies and
collections could be in no wise forwarded by a carriage
of this kind; moreover, that although by this means my
legs might get some ease, the other parts of me would
suffer for it in consequence of the jolting of the carriage;
therefore taking to my feet again, I went on till I arrived
at the company's farm.   The steward (or as they call

TRAVELLING BY OX-WAGGON.

him there, the *baas*) presented me with a glass of a strong-bodied wine, which was by no means adapted to quench my thirst; but the water here was brackish, and had a salt taste, and they had no milk nor cows, although there was upon the farm a considerable number of horses and other cattle. The reason of this was, that in such places there is usually stationed a guard of soldiers who care more for wine than milk; the pasture was likewise greatly in fault, being unfavourable for milch-cows, and drying up their milk. I therefore took leave of the *baas*, an appellation given to all the Christians here, particularly to bailiffs and farmers. The next farm belonged to a peasant, who was a native of Africa. I now took it into my head for the first time to make a trial of this people's so much boasted hospitality, but unluckily the man himself was gone to the review at the *Cape*, and had left only a few slaves at home under the command of an old Crone, who said that the bed-clothes were locked up. I could easily perceive that she had as little desire to harbour me, as I had to stay with her. It was now already dark, but notwithstanding this and my stiff and wearied legs, I resolved to go on to another farm-house that appeared in sight. We missed our way in a dale, and wandered among the thickets and bushes. The *jackals*, or African *foxes*, now began their nightly serenade, pretty much in the same notes as our foxes in Europe; frogs and owls filled up the concert with their horridly plaintive accompaniment. At length we came to a little rising ground, whence we could again discern the farm and discover the right road. A guard of dogs, which in Africa are allowed the unlimited privilege of falling foul on such foot-passengers of a night (the later the more liable to suspicion), set upon us, and frightened us not a little. It was now half an hour past eight; however, as the people

were not yet in bed, they came out to our assistance, so
that we received no other wounds than those inflicted on
the skirts of our coats.

51. OLD INHABITANTS OF SOUTH AFRICA.

I. The Antelopes.

COLONEL GORDON CUMMING.*

The springbok is so termed by the colonists on account
of its peculiar habit of springing, or taking extraordinary
bounds, rising to an incredible height in the air when
pursued.   The extraordinary manner in which springboks are capable of springing is best seen when they
are chased by a dog.   On these occasions away start the
herd with a succession of strange perpendicular bounds,
rising with curved loins high into the air, and at the
same time elevating the snowy folds of long white hair
on their haunches and along their backs, which imparts
to them a peculiar fairy-like appearance different from
any other animal.   They bound to the height of 10 or
12 feet with the elasticity of an indiarubber ball, clearing
at each spring from 12 to 15 feet of ground, without
apparently the slightest exertion.   In performing the
spring, they appear for an instant as if suspended in the
air, when down come all four feet again together, and,
striking the plain, away they soar again, as if about to
take flight.   The herd only adopt this motion for a few
hundred yards, when they subside into a light, elastic
trot, arching their graceful necks and lowering their noses
to the ground, as if in sportive mood.   Presently, pulling
up, they face about, and reconnoitre the object of their

* 'Five Years of a Hunter's Life.' (Murray, 1850.)

alarm. In crossing any path or waggon-road on which men have lately trod, the springbok invariably clears it by a single surprising bound ; and when a herd of perhaps many thousands have to cross a track of the sort, it is extremely beautiful to see how each antelope performs this feat, so suspicious are they of the ground on which their enemy, man, has trodden. They bound in a similar manner when passing to leeward of a lion or any other animal of which they entertain an instinctive dread.

The accumulated masses of living creatures which the springboks exhibit on the greater migrations is utterly astounding, and any traveller witnessing it as I have, and giving a true description of what he has seen, can hardly expect to be believed, so marvellous is the scene.

They have been well and truly compared to the wasting swarms of locusts so familiar to the traveller in this land of wonders. Like them, they consume every green thing in their course, laying waste vast districts in a few hours, and ruining in a single night the fruits of the farmer's toil. The course adopted by the antelopes is generally such as to bring them back to their own country by a route different from that by which they set out. Thus their line of march sometimes forms something like a vast oval, or an extensive square, of which the diameter may be some hundred miles, and the time occupied in this migration may vary from six months to a year.

*   *   *   *   *

I had the satisfaction of beholding, for the first time, what I had often heard the Boers allude to—viz., a ' trek-bokken,' or grand migration of springboks. This was, I think, the most extraordinary and striking scene, as connected with beasts of the chase, that I have ever beheld. For about two hours before the day dawned I had been

lying awake in my waggon, listening to the grunting of
the bucks within 200 yards of me, imagining that some
large herd of springboks was feeding beside my camp ;
but on my rising when it was clear, and looking about
me, I beheld the ground to the northward of my camp
actually covered with a dense living mass of springboks,
marching slowly and steadily along, extending from an
opening in a long range of hills on the west, through
which they continued pouring, like the flood of some
great river, to a ridge about a mile to the north-east,
over which they disappeared.

The breadth of the ground they covered might have
been somewhere about half a mile. I stood upon the
fore chest of my waggon for nearly two hours, lost in
wonder at the novel and wonderful scene which was
passing before me, and had some difficulty in convincing
myself that it was reality which I beheld, and not the
wild and exaggerated picture of a hunter's dream.
During this time their vast legions continued streaming
through the neck in the hills in one unbroken compact
phalanx.

*   *   *   *   *

52. OLD INHABITANTS OF SOUTH AFRICA.

II. The Bushmen.

A. SPARRMAN,* 1785.

There is another species of Hottentots, who have got
the name of *Boshies-men*, from dwelling in woody or mountainous places. These, particularly such as live round
about *Camdebo* and *Sneeberg*, are sworn enemies to the

* 'Voyage to the Cape,' 1785.

pastoral life. Some of their maxims are to live on
hunting and plunder, and never to keep any animal
alive for the space of one night. By this means they
render themselves odious to the rest of mankind, and are
pursued and exterminated like the wild beasts, whose
manners they have assumed. Others of them again are
kept alive and made slaves of.

Their weapons are poisoned arrows, which, shot out
of a small bow, will fly to the distance of two hundred
paces, and will hit a mark with a tolerable degree of
certainty at the distance of fifty or even a hundred paces.
From this distance they can by stealth, as it were, convey
death to the game they hunt for food, as well as to their
foes, and even to so large and tremendous a beast as the
lion; this noble animal thus falling by a weapon which,
perhaps, it despised, or even did not take notice of. The
Hottentot, in the mean time, concealed and safe in his
ambush, is absolutely certain of the operation of his
poison, which he always culls of the most virulent kind;
and it is said he has only to wait a few minutes in order
to see the wild beast languish and die.

    *   *   *   *   *

A great many of them are entirely naked, but such as
have been able to procure the skin of any sort of animal,
great or small, cover their bodies with it from the
shoulders downwards as far as it will reach, wearing
it till it falls off their backs in rags. As ignorant of
agriculture as apes and monkeys, like them they are
obliged to wander about over hills and dales after certain
wild roots, berries, and plants (which they eat raw) in
order to sustain a life that this miserable food would
soon extinguish and destroy, were they used to better
fare.

Their table, however, is sometimes composed of several

other dishes, among which may be reckoned the larvæ of insects, or those kind of caterpillars from which butter-flies are generated; and in like manner a sort of white ants (the *termes*), grasshoppers, snakes, and some sorts of spiders. With all these changes of diet, the *Boshies-man* is, nevertheless, frequently in want, and famished to such a degree as to waste almost to a shadow. It was with no small astonishment that I for the first time saw in *Lange Kloof* a lad belonging to this race of men, with his face, arms, legs and body so monstrously small and withered, that I could not have been induced to suppose but that he had been brought to that state by the fever that was epidemic in those parts, had I not seen him at the same time run like a lapwing.

53. THE KALAHARI DESERT.

COLONEL GORDON CUMMING.*

The country looked very unlikely for water, and the Bechuanas swore that there was none for seven days' journey in that direction. Our march lay through a boundless forest, with no hill or landmark to give me an idea where to search for water. Fortune, however, followed me here as usual; if I had lived all my life in the country I could not have taken a more direct course for the spot I wished to reach. After we had proceeded some miles, a rising ground arose in our path, from the summit of which I fancied that a view might be obtained of the country in advance. This view only served to damp my hopes, the prospect exhibiting one slightly undulating, ocean‑like expanse of forest and dense thorny jungles. We halted for a few minutes to breathe

* 'Five Years of a Hunter's Life.'

the oxen, when the Bechuanas all came up, and sat
down on the ground beside us. I asked them why they
had not gone home as I had told them. They replied
that they followed me because they were afraid that I
should lose myself and my oxen.

We held on, steering by compass N.N.E. All the
Bechuanas now forsook me, except the four ill-favoured
men whom Caachy had pointed out to me as my guides.
These four, contrary to my expectations, followed in our
wake at some distance. I walked a hundred yards in
advance of the waggons with my compass in my hand,
having ordered the men to follow my footsteps. After
travelling for several hours, the country became more
open, and presently we entered upon a wide tract that
had been recently burned by the Bakalahari, or wild
inhabitants of the desert. Here the trees and bushes
stood scorched and burnt, and there was not a blade
of grass to cheer the eye; blackness and ashes stretched
away on every side wherever I turned my anxious glance.
I felt my heart sink within me as I beheld in dim perspective my famished and thirsty oxen returning some
days hence over this hopeless desert, all my endeavours
to find water having failed, and all my bright hopes of
elephant-hunting dashed and crowned with bitter disappointment; it was, indeed, a bitter prospect. I had
no friend to comfort or advise me, and I could hear my
men behind me grumbling, and swearing that they would
return home, the guides, who had now come up, asking
them why they followed me to destruction.

At length we reached the farther side of this dreary
waste of ashes, but now an equally cheerless prospect
was before me. We entered a vast forest, gray with
extreme age, and so thick that we could not see forty
yards in advance. We were obliged occasionally to halt

the waggons and cut down trees and branches to admit
of their passing; and to make matters still worse, the
country had become extremely heavy, the waggons
sinking deep in soft sand. My men began to show a
mutinous spirit by expressing their opinions aloud in my
presence. I remonstrated with them, and told them that
if I did not bring them to water next day before the sun
was under, they might turn the oxen on their spoor.
We continued our march through this dense forest until
nightfall, when I halted for the night beside a wide-
spreading tree; here I cast my oxen loose for an hour,
and then secured them on the yokes by moonlight. . . .

I went to bed, but tried in vain to sleep. Care and
anxiety kept me awake until a little before morning,
when I fell asleep for a short time, and dreamt that I
had ridden in advance and found water. Day dawned,
and I awoke in sorrow. My hopes were like a flickering
flame; care sat upon my brow. . . .

I asked the guides if they could lead me to water in a
northerly direction, when they replied that no man ever
found water in the desert. I did not talk more with
them, but ordered my men to remain quiet during the
day and listen for shots, lest I should lose my way in
returning; and having given them ammunition to reply,
I saddled up and held N.N.E. through thick forest,
accompanied by Kleinboy. The ground was heavy,
being soft sand, and the grass grew at intervals in
detached bunches. We rode on without a break or a
change, and found no spoor of wild animals to give me
hope. I saw one duiker, but these antelopes are met
with in the desert, and are independent of water.

At last we reached a more open part of the forest, and
emerging from the thicket, I perceived a troop of six or
eight beautiful giraffes, standing looking at us about

200 yards to my right; but this was no time to give
them chase, which I felt very much inclined to do. I
allowed them to depart in peace, and continued my
search for water. In this open glade I found two or
three vleys that had once contained a little water, but
they were now hard and dry. Re-entering the dense
forest, we held one point more to the east, and rode on
as before. For miles we continued our search, until my
hopes sank to a very low ebb, and Kleinboy swore that
we should never regain the waggons. At length I
perceived a sassayby walking before me; this antelope
drinks every day. 'Fresh vigour with the hope returned.'
I once more pressed forward and cantered along, heed-
less of the distance which already intervened betwixt me
and my camp and the remonstrances of my attendant,
who at last reined up his jaded steed, and said that he
would not follow me farther to my own destruction. I
then pointed to the top of a distant gray tree that
stretched its bare and weather-beaten branches above
the heads of its surrounding comrades, and said that if
we saw nothing to give us hope when we reached that
tree, I would abandon the search. . . .

But fate had ordained that I should penetrate farther
into the interior of Africa, and before I reached the old
gray tree I observed a small flight of Namaqua par-
tridges flying across my path in a westerly direction. It
was impossible to tell, until I should see a second flock
of these, flying at a different angle, whether the first
flock had come from, or were going to, water. For this
I accordingly watched, nor watched long in vain. A
considerable distance ahead of me I detected a second
flight of these birds likewise flying westerly, and it was
evident, from their inclination, that they held for the
same point as the first had done. Shortly afterwards

the first flight returned, flying high above our heads, uttering their soft, melodious cry of ' Pretty dear, pretty dear !' I then rode in the direction from which the birds had come, and before proceeding far we discovered a slight hollow running north and south.   This I determined to follow, and presently I discovered fresh spoor of a rhinoceros; this was a certain sign that water was somewhere not very distant.

Once more my dying hopes revived. I looked north at the glorious sky, which on this particular day was quite different from anything I had beheld for months. It was like one of those glorious days when the bright blue sky in my own dark land is seen through ten thousand joyous fleecy clouds, and all nature seems to strive in its sunny hour to make poor unhappy man forget his cares and sorrows. I took it as a favourable omen, and, stirring my good and lively steed, I cantered along the glade. The hollow took a turn, on rounding which I perceived that I was in an elevated part of the forest, and I, for the first time, obtained a different view of the surrounding scenery.   Far as the eye could strain, it was all forest without a break, but there was now an undulating country before me instead of the hopeless level through which I had come.   I felt certain of success. We soon discovered vleys that had recently contained water, and at last a large pool of excellent water, enough to supply my cattle for several days.

*   *   *   *   *

54. THE RUINS IN SOUTH AFRICA (A PORTUGUESE ACCOUNT).

'PURCHAS—HIS PILGRIMES,' 1625.

Near to *Massapa* is a great high Hill, called *Fura*, whence may be discerned a great part of the Kingdom of *Manamotapa :* for which cause he will not suffer the *Portugalls* to go thither that they should not covet his great Country and hidden Mines. On the top of that Hill are yet standing pieces of old walls and ancient ruines of lime and stone, which testify that there have been strong buildings: a thing not seen in all *Cafraria.* For the King's houses are of wood, daubed with clay, and covered with straw.

The Natives, and specially the *Moores*, have a Tradition from their Ancestors that those houses belonged to the Queen of *Saba*, which carried much Gold thence down the *Cuama* to the Sea, and so along the Coast of *Æthiopia* to the Red Sea. Others say that those Ruins were *Solomon's* Factory, and that this *Fura* or *Afura* is no other then *Ophir*, the name not much altered in so long time. This is certain, that round about that hill there is much and fine Gold. The Navigation might in those times be longer, for want of so good ships and Pilots as now are to be had, and by reason of much time spent in trucking with the Cafars, wherein even at this time the Merchants always spend a year and more in that business, although the *Cafars* be grown more covetous of our Wares, and the Mines better known. They are so lazy to gather the Gold that they will not do it till necessity constrains them. Much time is also spent in the Voyage by the Rivers, and by that Sea which hath differing Monsoons, and can be sailed but by two winds, which blow six months from the East, and as many from the West.

Solomon's fleet had, besides those mentioned, this let, that the Red Sea is not safely Navigable but in the day, by reason of many Isles and shoals; likewise it was necessary often to put to harbour for fresh water and other provisions, and to take in new Pilots and Mariners, and to make reparations, which, considered (*with their creeping by shore for want of the Compass and experience in those Seas, and their Sabbath rests, and their truck with the* Cafres) might extend the whole Voyage in going, staying, and returning, to three years.   Further, the Ivory, Apes, Gems, and precious woods (which grow in the wild places of *Tebe*, within *Sofala*), whence they make *Almadias* or *Canoas* twenty yards long of one Timber; and much fine black wood (*Ebonie*) grows in that coast, and is thence carried to *India* and *Portugall:* all these may make the matter probable.   As for Peacocks, I saw none there, but there must needs be some within Land; for I have seen some *Cafars* wear their Plumes on their heads. And as there is store of fine Gold, so also is there fine silver in *Chicoua*, where are rich Minès.

In all the Regions of *Manamotapa*, or the greatest part thereof, are many Mines of Gold; and particularly in *Chiroro*, where is the most and most fine.   It is pain of death for any *Moore* which discovers a Mine to take away any, besides his goods forfeited to the King.   And if by chance any find a Mine, he is bound to cry out aloud that some other *Cafar* may come to testify that he takes none; and both are then to cover the place with Earth, and set a great bough thereon, to give warning to other *Cafars* to avoid the place.   For if they should come there it would cost them their lives, although there be no proof that he took anything.   This severity is used to keep the Mines from

the knowledge of the *Portugals*, lest covetous desire
thereof might cause them to take away their Country.
It is found in powder like sand ; in grains like beads; in
pieces, some smooth as they were melted, others branched
with snags, others mixed so with Earth, that the Earth
being well washed from them, they remain like *Honie-
combs ;* those holes, before full of red earth, seeming as
though they were also to be turned into Gold.

55. ZIMBABWE, AS REPORTED BY THE DUTCH.

DAPPER, 1670.

In this Country, far to the inland on a Plain, in the
middle of many Iron-Mills, stands a famous structure,
called Simbaoe, built square like a Castle, with hewn
Stone of a wonderful bigness; the Walls are more than
five and twenty Foot broad, but the height not answer-
able ; above the Gate appears an Inscription, which cannot be read or understood, nor could any that have seen
it know what people used such Letters. . . .

The inhabitants report it a work of the Devil, themselves only building with wood, and aver that for strength
it exceeds the Fort of the *Portuguese* at the Sea-shore,
about a hundred and fifty miles from thence.

56. ZIMBABWE EXPLORED.

J. THEODORE BENT,[*] 1891.

The prominent features of the Great Zimbabwe ruins,
which cover a large area of ground, are, firstly, the large
circular ruin, with its round tower on the edge of a gentle

* ' Ruined Cities of Mashonaland.' (Longmans, 1893.)

slope on the plain below; secondly, the mass of ruins in
the valley immediately beneath this; and thirdly, the
intricate fortress on the granite hill above, acting as the
acropolis of the ancient city. . . .

When we reached the Great Zimbabwe, the circular
ruin was on the inside a dense mass of tropical vegetation; creepers and monkey-ropes hung in matted con-
fusion to the tall trees, forming a jungle which it was
almost impossible to penetrate, and added to the mazy
labyrinth of walls a peculiar and almost awe-inspiring
mystery.

    *   *   *   *   *

As for the walls themselves, they were nearly free
from vegetation, for, owing to the absence of mortar, no
lichen, moss, nor creeper could thrive on them, and those
few things which had penetrated into crevices were of a
succulent character, which formed their branches to the
shape of the interstices. To this fact is due the wonderful state of preservation in which these ruins are found.

    *   *   *   *   *

Such is the great fortress of Zimbabwe, the most
mysterious and complex structure that it has ever been
my fate to look upon. Vainly one tries to realize what it
must have been like in the days before ruin fell upon it,
with its tortuous and well-guarded approaches, its walls
bristling with monoliths and round towers, its temple
decorated with tall, weird-looking birds, its huge decorated
bowls, and in the innermost recesses its busy gold-pro-
ducing furnace. What was this life like? Why did the
inhabitants so carefully guard themselves against attack?
A thousand questions occur to one which one longs in
vain to answer. The only parallel sensation that I have
had was when viewing the long avenues of menhirs, near
Carnac in Brittany, a sensation at once fascinating and

vexatious, for one feels the utter hopelessness of knowing all one would wish on the subject. When taken alone, this fortress is sufficiently a marvel; but when taken together with the large circular building below, the numerous ruins scattered around, the other ruins of a like nature at a distance, one cannot fail to recognise the vastness and power of this ancient race, their great constructive ingenuity and strategic skill.

57. GOLD AND DIAMOND MINING TO-DAY.

SIR F. YOUNG, K.C.M.G.,* 1890.

To anyone visiting for the first time this great centre of the diamond industry of South Africa, the scene is most extraordinary. The excitement and bustle, the wild whirl of vehicular traffic, the fearful dust, the ceaseless movement of men and women of all descriptions, and of every shade of complexion and colour, are positively bewildering. The thoughts of everybody appear to be centred in diamonds, and the prevailing talk and speech are accordingly. Being the recipient, myself, of the most kind attention and genial and generous hospitality, my stay was most agreeable and pleasant. Great facilities were afforded me for seeing everything connected with this wonderful industry, and satisfying myself that there are no present signs of its being exhausted or 'played out.' Indubitable evidences were given me that diamonds continue to be found in as large quantities as ever. They appeared to me to be 'as plentiful as blackberries.'

At the Bultfontein Mine I descended to the bottom of the open workings in one of the iron buckets, used for

* 'A Winter Tour in South Africa.' (Petherick, 1890.)

bringing up the 'blue ground' to the surface. This is rather a perilous adventure. To go down by a wire rope, some 500 or 600 feet, perpendicular into the bowels of the earth with lightning rapidity, standing up in an open receptacle, the top of which does not approach your waist, oscillating like a pendulum, while you are holding on 'like grim death' by your hands, is something more than a joke. It certainly ought not to be attempted by anyone who does not possess a cool head and tolerable nerve.

Here I saw multitudes of natives employed—as afterwards in the De Beer's, the Kimberley, and other diamond-mines—with pickaxes, shovels, and other tools, breaking down the ground at the sides of the mine, perched at various spots, and many a giddy height. Diamond - mining at Kimberley is altogether a very wonderful specimen of the development of a new industry. In this mine I had explained to me the various processes by which diamonds are discovered in the rocky strata which is being constantly dug out of the enormous circular hole constituting it.

I also visited the celebrated De Beer's Mine. This vast mine, where some thousands of workmen, white and coloured, are employed, is carried on much in the same way as the Bultfontein, as far as the different processes are concerned, of treating the material in which the diamonds are found. It is much richer, however, in 'blue ground,' and consequently far more valuable results are obtained from it. For instance, the average value of each truck-load of stuff from the Bultfontein is said to be about 8s., while from the De Beer's it is 28s. or 30s. The latter mine is now worked underground, in the same way as copper and coal-mines are worked in England. Excellent arrangements are made for the protection and

well-being of the native workmen, especially by the
introduction of 'compounds' during the last year or two.
These are vast enclosures, with high walls, where the
natives compulsorily reside after their daily work is done
during the whole time they remain at work in the mine.
This system has been attended with the most satisfactory results. I went over the De Beer's 'compound,'
where I saw an immense number of natives, all appearing
lively, cheerful, and happy. A large number were playing
at cards (they are great gamblers), and others amusing
themselves in various ways. No intoxicating liquor is
permitted to be sold within the 'compounds.' The
weekly receipts for ginger-beer amount to a sum which
seems fabulous, averaging from £60 to £100 a week.
The natives can purchase from the 'compound' store
every possible thing they want, from a tin pot to a
blanket, from a suit of old clothes to a pannikin of
mealies. Before the establishment of the 'compounds,'
when the natives had the free run of the town, and could
obtain alcoholic liquor—on Saturday nights especially,
after they had done their work and received their weekly
wages—Kimberley was a perfect pandemonium.

Johannesburg.

This 'auriferous' town is indeed a marvellous place,
lying on the crest of a hill at an elevation of 5,000 feet
above the level of the sea. Along its sides are spread
out every variety of habitation, from the substantial brick
and stone structures, which are being erected with extraordinary rapidity, to the multitude of galvanized iron
dwellings, and the still not unfrequent tents of the first
and last comers. It is, indeed, a wonderful and bewildering sight to view it from the opposite hill across

the intervening valley. Scarcely more than two years
have elapsed since this town of 25,000 inhabitants
commenced its miraculous existence. The excitement
and bustle of the motley crowd of gold-seekers and gold-
finders is tremendous the whole of the livelong day.
The incessant subject of all conversation is gold, gold,
gold. It is in all their thoughts, excepting, perhaps, a
too liberal thought of drink. The people of Johannesburg think of gold; they talk of gold; they dream of
gold. I believe, if they could, they would eat and drink
gold. But, demoralizing as this is to a vast number of
those who are in the vortex of the daily doings of this
remarkable place, the startling fact is only too apparent
to anyone who visits Johannesburg. It is to be hoped
that the day will come when the legitimate pursuit of
wealth will be followed in a less excitable and a more
calm and decorous manner than at present regrettably
prevails.

58. THE VICTORIA FALLS.

J. CHAPMAN, 1862.*

When we halted for the night, under a huge motsèbe
tree by the path-side, we had no idea we were so near
the ' Falls,' but as the boisterous laughter and merry
frolicking of our little Makalakas subsided, there gradually
arose in the air a murmuring, and at length a roaring
sound, increasing as the night advanced, and sounding
like the dashing of a mighty surf upon a rock-bound
coast. So much does the sound resemble this that a
stranger, unacquainted with the existence of a waterfall
here, and unaware of his distance from the sea, could not
be persuaded to the contrary. It was one everlasting

* ' Travels in the Interior of Africa.' (Stanford, 1868.)

roar, broken occasionally by the thundering, like successive cannonading in the distance ; and thus it sounded
all through the night.

Next morning I walked on, in the hopes of falling in
with a buffalo, or some other game, when, on rounding
the point of the high sandy ridge on which we slept, my
attention was attracted by some object shining through
the forest in the distance. That must be water, I men-
tally exclaimed, as, with some difficulty, I ascended a
tree, and there beheld, at the distance of some six miles,
a long line of smoking clouds, five large and a great
many smaller ones, rising perpendicularly from a crack
in the earth, as if from a vigorously burning fire, the
flames alone being wanting to render the picture perfect.
But now the sun rose, shining brightly upon the waters,
and gradually dispelling the sombre hues of the huge
columns of floating vapours, some of which rose to the
height of upwards of 100 feet, imparting to them a
warmer, lighter, and more gauzy aspect, which enabled
me at once to see the water behind the columns in the
background, and that I was in reality facing the Victoria
Falls. As the sun sparkled on the edge of the precipice,
I could distinctly see the water falling into a long, dark,
and narrow chasm, out of which the columns of smoke
arose. The course of the river from the north-west was
to be distinguished by a long and broad sheet of silvery
water, which, running from between low hills, had at
this distance the appearance of a placid lake, studded
with little palm islands. On the south side, again, a
double line of sunlit waters shone in the depths of a
beautifully wooded valley on our right, groups of dark,
umbrageous trees stood out in bold relief, casting their
lengthy shadows over the grassy plains beneath, looking
like so many graves with tombstones at their heads. In

the immediate foreground were tops of naked almond trees, and I recognised, to my astonishment, the anna-boom (of Damara Land), known here as moku.

We now ascended another hill, the last which im-peded our way, on reaching the summit of which we got a fine view of the whole length of the face of the ' Falls,' and an abrupt acclivitous gorge on our right, evidently the opposite bank of the Zambesi river, having a per-pendicular wall of rock of gigantic height, winding in a zigzag manner, and becoming bolder towards the east end of the ' Falls.'

On a nearer approach, the river became visible, running from the north-west ; and as far as we could see—some two miles—it was studded with numerous islands, covered with clustering groups of palms and evergreens.

In so far as we could ascertain, there was no possibility of seeing the whole at once from any point on this side, saving the bird's-eye view I had obtained in the morning; for if the trees and surrounding objects did not exclude the view from the eye, the clouds of vapour arising out of the fissure beneath would effectually do so within the first quarter of a mile.

We descended for twenty minutes from the side of a sloping hill, rising probably 300 feet above the 'Falls,' through a forest which quite excluded the view, excepting the vapour, until we stood on the brink at the one end. . . .

We approached the brink with trembling, and, care-fully parting the bushes with our hands, looked at once on the first grand view of the ' Falls ' at the west end. Picture to yourself a stupendous perpendicular rent in a mass of basaltic rock, extending more than a mile (scarcely the half of which, however, is visible), and only 60 to 100 or 120 yards wide, right across the river, from one end to the other, into which pours this mighty river, roaring, foaming, and boiling. Then immediately before you a large body of water, between 80 and 90 yards wide, stealing at first with rapid and snake-like undulations over the hard and slippery rock, at length leaping at an angle of 30°, then 45°, for more than 100 yards, and then, with the impetus its rapid descent has given it, bounding bodily 15 or 20 feet clear of the rock, and falling with thundering report into the dark and boiling chasm beneath, seeming, by its velocity, so to entrance the nervous spectator that he fancies himself being involuntarily drawn into the stream, and by some invisible spell tempted to fling himself headlong into it and join in its gambols; but anon he recovers himself with a nervous start, and draws back a pace or two, gazing in awe and wonder upon the stream as it goes leaping wildly, and with 'delirious bound,' over huge rocks. It is a scene of wild sublimity.

On the opposite cliff of this channel star-like aloes, with scarlet blossoms, cluster against the sides of the deep brown rock; and beyond that we look into a dark and misty cavern, the depths of which we could not see. Three pretty snowy rills, enveloped in sylvan vegetation, fall, ghost-like, through the veil of mist, and disappear down this dark cave, the fit abode of Nox and Erebus. Beyond this we see a projection of bare brown rock, over which no water falls, and then a perspective of white and fleecy waters, falling like snowy avalanches, slipping from an abrupt precipice into clouds of ascending mist. . . .

We lingered at this spot until the sun was long past its meridian, the deep gulf before us rolling up large, dense clouds of spray, on which the sun at our back, shining full on it, reflects two, sometimes three, lovely

VICTORIA FALLS ON THE ZAMBESI.

bows, spanning their brilliant arches, first in the depth of the chasm, but at length rising higher and higher, and forming a double archway across the gigantic walls of the fissure. Rainbows so bright, so vivid are never seen in the skies. The lower one in particular, probably from the contrast with the black-looking rocks below, was *too* vivid, nay, almost blinding to look upon, defying imitation by the most skilful artist, and all the colours at his command, yet imparting its heavenly tints to every object over which it successively passes. The colours in these ' rainbows ' are reversed, the upper one being blue, yellow, and red, the lower red, yellow, and blue. As the sun declined, the rainbows ascended, until they reached the clouds of spray above the horizon. One segment of the bows is cut off where the spray ends, but the other end is still rising higher and increasing in depth, and as you retreat a little, it spans the whole river for fully a mile, imparting the most lovely colour to the spray-clouds, which steal aloft like tongues of sulphur flame, until lost to view by the downward course of the sun; then the second and more vivid rainbow takes its place and goes through the same evolutions, enlivening and beautifying the scene in the most remarkable manner.

It was necessary to proceed farther to obtain a more extended view, so making a circuit of about fifty yards to get round the steep sloping thicket at the west end of the fissure, we peered into it as far as we might, but saw only a profusion of vines, aloes, and evergreens bathed in moisture, and creeping and clinging along its steep sides where man may not venture, their leaves sparkling and glistening with the constant shower. Having rounded this point, we approached the brink of the south cliff, and putting aside the small date-palms, now faced the leaping waters in their headlong course. The sun,

shining on its upper surface, rendered it like quicksilver,
painful to look upon.   We approached the wet and
slippery brink in a perpetual shower of rain, and, holding on to one another, looked down into the awful chasm
beneath us.   One look for me is enough, but my nerves
are sorely tried by Baines, who, finding everywhere new
beauties for his pencil, must needs drag me along the
very edge, he gazing with delight, I with terror, down
into the lowest depths of the chasm.   We continued
along the grassy bank, preceded by numerous lovely little
rainbows spanning round us, a forest to our right, the
chasm on our left, until at length, not wishing to see any
more at present, but gradually to accustom myself to the
stupefying effects of the uproar and tumult at work in
this ' cauldron,' I fairly fled from my companion.

We now passed on again through the forest, collecting
specimens of ferns, fungi, and polypi, which we had
never seen before.   We see the scenery at a great dis-
advantage just now, as this is the time of the ' sere and
yellow leaf.'   The principal verdure is furnished by evergreens, and there are enough of them ; but there are at
present no flowers, saving the scarlet blossoms of the
aloe clustering against the brown wall of the fissure.

Before leaving this swampy spot I must not omit to
mention the fact that to our amazement we found
numerous spoors of elephants, rhinoceroses, buffaloes,
and hippopotami, besides other animals, all over the very
brink of the precipice.   It makes one's hair stand on end
to see the numerous indications of their midnight rambles
at the very verge of eternity.   Here they come at the
dead dark midnight hour to drink the spray and wallow
in the mire, and on asking a native how it was they were
not afraid, he asked me in return : ' Didn't they grow up
together ? '

[59. BRITISH CENTRAL AFRICA.

SIR H. H. JOHNSTON.*

For the trader and the planter I think it may be said
that the country offers sufficiently sure and rapid profits
for their enterprise to compensate the risk run in the
matter of health. The various trading companies in the
country appear to be doing well with an ever-extending
business, and to be constantly increasing the number of
their establishments. Even traders in a small way, if
they have energy and astuteness, may reap considerable
earnings with relatively small outlay. One man, for
instance, went up to Kotakota, on Lake Nyassa, with a
few hundreds of pounds at his disposal, bought a large
number of cattle at a very low price in the Marimba district, and purchased all the ivory the Arabs at Kotakota
had to dispose of, and on his total transaction made a
clear profit of £2,000 by selling the cattle and ivory at
Blantyre ; but it appears to me that as time goes on
the European trading community will be limited to the
employés of two or three great trading companies com-
manding considerable capital, and to a number of British
Indians who will not in any way conflict with the commerce of the Europeans because they will often act as
the middlemen, buying up small quantities of produce
here and there from the natives which they will re-sell in
large amounts to the European firms and agencies.

The remainder of the European settlers will be rather
planters than traders, disposing likewise of their produce
to the commercial companies in British Central Africa.
Originally, when there was very little or no cash in the
country, every planter had likewise to be a trader on a

* ' British Central Africa.' (Methuen, 1897.)

small scale, as all labourers were paid in trade goods,
and all the food that he bought from the natives was
purchased in the same manner. Now the country is full
of cash, and in many districts the natives refuse to accept
any payment except in money, preferring to go to the
principal stores and make their purchases there. To a
certain extent, moreover, money payments are now com-
pulsory between European employers and their native
employés; moreover, a planter often objects to taking
out a trading license, and prefers instead to relinquish
his small commerce in this respect.

Briefly stated, the only serious drawback to British
Central Africa as a field of enterprise for trader or
planter is malarial fever, either in its ordinary form,
or in its severest type.

> *   *   *   *   *

I shall have a few words to say about this malady
further on. The advantages are, at the present time,
that land is cheap; the country is almost everywhere
well watered by perennial streams, and by a reasonable
rainfall; the scenery is beautiful in many of the upland
districts; the climate is delicious—seldom too hot, and
often cold and pleasant; there is an abundance of cheap
native labour; transport, though offering certain difficulties inherent in all undeveloped parts of Africa, is growing
far easier and cheaper than in Central South Africa, as
the Shire river is navigable at all times of the year,
except for about eighty miles of its course; and Lake
Nyassa is an inland sea, with a shore-line of something like
800 miles. Moreover, the cost of simple articles of food,
such as oxen, goats or sheep, or of antelopes and other
big game, poultry, eggs, and milk, is cheap, together with
the prices of a few vegetables like potatoes, or grain like
Indian corn; and all the European goods are not so

expensive as they would be in the interior of Australia, in Central South Africa, or in the interior of South America, because of the relative cheapness of transport from the coast, and of the very low Customs duties.

To sum up the question, I might state with truth that *but* for malarial fever this country would be an earthly paradise; the ' but,' however, is a very big one. Whether the development of medical science will enable us to find the same antidote to malarial fever as we have found for small-pox in vaccination, or whether drugs will be discovered which will make the treatment of the disease and recovery therefrom almost certain, remains to be seen. If however here, as in other parts of tropical Africa, this demon could be conjured, beyond all question the prosperity of Western Africa, of the Congo Basin, and of British Central Africa would be almost unbounded.

PART VI.

THE CONGO.

INTRODUCTION.

THE Congo, which pours into the sea a greater flood than any stream in the world except the Amazon, is by far the largest of the African rivers ; but, unlike the Nile and the Niger, it has had no history until modern times. When we trace its majestic course on a map of Africa, it is hard to realize that the very existence of this mighty stream, with its wide-circling sweep across the equator, was, when the last quarter of the nineteenth century began, not merely unknown, but scarcely even suspected. The Congo forms no delta, so that its wide mouth and the strong current issuing from it could not escape the notice of the first navigators who passed that way (see 30) ; but for nearly four hundred years after their discovery little else was discovered. The first serious attempt to ascend it was made in 1816 by the expedition under Captain Tuckey, the members of which, as has already been said, believed themselves to be ascending the Niger. The explorers, whose terrible sufferings and losses did not bring the Congo climate into good odour with the world, ascended the stream for about 150 miles, when they were stopped by impassable cataracts; and 'Tuckey's furthest' was the limit of all that was certainly known about the Congo for more than half a century after their time.

The great explorer who threw new light upon its upper course did so without his knowledge and almost against his will. Early in his career Dr. Livingstone, during his celebrated journey across the continent, came upon the upper waters of the Kasai, which is one of the Congo's largest southern tributaries, and might, for anything that was then known, have turned out to be the main river itself. But during the journeys that occupied the last years of his life Livingstone made the exciting discovery that a river of no great size, called the Chambeze, rising far away on the eastern side of the continent, near Lake Nyassa, passed through two considerable lakes to pour itself into the waters of a very large river, named the Lualaba, which flowed in a northerly direction, no one knew whither, through the country west of Tanganyika. In this river Livingstone believed that he had found the true head-stream of the Nile, into which he supposed it to find an entrance by way of Baker's Albert Nyanza, the southern shores of which were as yet unexplored. It was while working out this question that Livingstone, who had been for some time quite lost to the world, was discovered by Sir H. M. Stanley, who had gone out in search of him, and he had not completed his work when death overtook him on the shores of Lake Bangweolo.

There are passages in Livingstone's diary which show that he had misgivings at times lest his new river might after all turn out to be, not the historic Nile, but the neglected Congo. And that this was the truth became clear to the next explorer (Cameron) as he stood on the banks of the mighty stream at Nyangwe, and perceived that it was even here a much larger river than the Upper Nile, into which Livingstone had supposed it to flow. The only outlet by which so vast a body of water could be poured into the ocean must evidently be the far-distant mouth of the Congo.

To reach this outlet the river takes a longer course than Cameron can have suspected. Unable to procure means of navigating its waters, he turned to the west, and succeeded in reaching the coast near Benguela, several hundreds of miles south of the Congo mouth, without ever meeting the river again. Then came one of the most remarkable journeys in the history of exploration, when Stanley, embarking a large train of followers in canoes on the Lualaba, was borne away on the great stream far to the north of the equator, curving back again, after many adventures with cannibals and with cataracts, to reach the point to which Tuckey had ascended sixty years before. The discovery of the Congo Valley revealed a new African world, and began a new and surprising chapter in African history. Years have been spent in exploring the many large rivers that on both sides pour themselves into the gigantic stream.

All, or almost all, great rivers are known by different names at different places to the people who dwell along their banks, so that the name by which the world agrees to call any such river is generally the name originally of only one part of it. The name by which we know the Congo, however, never really belonged to any part of it. At its mouth it seems to have been first called Zaire (see 60), but it was known as the river of Congo from the territory through which it flowed into the sea. Stanley endeavoured (see 66) to fix upon the whole river the name of Livingstone, but his proposal has not been adopted.

60. THE CONGO MOUTH.

DAPPER.[*]

The River of Zair breaks forth with an opening above
3 Leagues in breadth, in the elevation of 5 degrees and
40 minutes, and with so great force and abundance of
water runs into the sea, that the fresh stream coming
out west-north-west and north-east and by north makes
an impression therein above 12 Leagues; and when you
are out of sight of land, yet the Water appears black,
and full of heaps of Reeds, and other things, like little
floating Islands, which the force of the Stream, pouring
from high Cliffs, tears out of the Countrey, and throws
into the Ocean, so that the Seamen, without a stiff Gale
of Wind, can hardly sail through it, to get into the Road
within *Padron*, on the south side of the River.

This violent and precipitate descent carries the Stream
against you 14 or 15 miles.   It sends forth on both sides
many Branches or Rivers, to the great convenience both
of the Inhabitants and foreign Tradesmen, who thereby
in Boats and Canoos pass from one Town to another.
In the Towns seated on these outstretched Arms dwell
People small of stature, probably Pigmies.

61. AN EARLY ATTEMPT TO ASCEND THE CONGO.

CAPTAIN J. K. TUCKEY, 1816.[†]

Both sides of the river appeared to be lined by rocks
above water, and the middle obstructed by whirlpools,
whose noise we heard in a constant roar, just where our
view terminated by the closing in of the points.   High

[*] Ogilvy's translation, 1670.
[†] 'Narrative' (Murray, 1818).

breakers seemed to cross the river; and this place we
learnt was called Casan Yellala, or Yellala's Wife, and
were told that no canoe ever attempted to pass it. The
most distant hill, whose summit appeared above the rest
at the distance of perhaps seven or eight leagues, we
found was that of Yellala. The appearance of the river
here was compared by Dr. Smith to the torrent rivers of
Norway, and particularly the Glommen, the hills on each
side being high, precipitous towards the river, totally
barren, and separated by such deep ravines as to preclude
the idea of conveying even a canoe over them without
immense labour. Two tufts of trees on the summits of
the northern hills, we understood from a fisherman, were
the plantations round the banzas. The only other information we could get from him was that Yellala was
the residence of the evil spirit, and that whoever saw it
once would never see it a second time.

This has been the only tolerable clear day since our
entering the river; the sun being visible both at rising
and setting, and the thermometer at two o'clock at 80°.
This heat produced a breeze in the evening stronger than
any we before experienced, and which continued all night.
On a little sand beach, off which the boats were anchored,
there is a regular rise and fall of water of 8 inches; during
the rise the current is considerably slackened.

August 13.—This morning at daylight I went up the
river with the master in the gigs, to ascertain the utility
of carrying the boats any farther. By crossing over from
shore to shore, as the current was found slackest, we
found no difficulty in getting up to Casan Yellala, which
is about three miles above where the boats lay. We
found it to be a ledge of rocks stretching across the north
shore about two-thirds the breadth of the river (which
here does not exceed half a mile), the current breaking

furiously on it, but leaving a smooth channel near the south shore, where the velocity of the current seems the only obstacle to the ascent of boats, and that I should consider as none to my progress with the boats did there appear to be the smallest utility in getting them above it. But as the shore on either side presents the most stupendous overhanging rocks, to whose crags alone the boats could be secured, while an impetuous current flows beneath ; and as every information makes Yellala a cataract of great perpendicular fall, to which the approach is far easiest from the place near which the boats are now anchored in perfect safety, I determined to visit this cataract by land, in order to determine on my future operations.

Accordingly, at eight o'clock on the morning of the fourteenth, I landed on the north shore, in a cove with a fine sandy beach, covered with the dung of the hippopotamus, exactly resembling that of the horse. My party consisted of Messrs. Smith, Tudor, Galwey, and Hodder, and thirteen men, besides two Embomma interpreters (the Chenoo's sons), and a guide from Noki, with four days' provisions. Our route lay by narrow footpaths, at first over most difficult hills, and then along a level plateau of fertile land ; in short, over a country resembling that between the river and Noki. Our course lay between E.N.E. and N.E. At noon we reached Banza Cooloo, from whence we understood we should see Yellala. Anxious to get a sight of it, I declined the Chenoo's invitation to visit him until my return. On the farthest end of the banza we unexpectedly saw the fall almost under our feet, and were not less surprised than disappointed at finding, instead of a second Niagara, which the description of the natives and their horror of it had given us, reason to expect, a comparative brook bubbling over its stony bed. Halting the people, who complained of fatigue, I went with the gentlemen to examine it more closely, and found that what the road wanted in distance, which was not a mile from the banza, it abundantly made up in difficulty, having one enormous hill to descend and a lesser one to climb, to reach the precipice which overhangs the river.

The south side of the river is here a vast hill of bare rock (sienite), and the north a lower but more precipitous hill of the same substance, between which two the river has forced its course ; but in the middle an island of slate still defies its power, and breaks the current into two narrow channels ; that near the south side gives vent to the great mass of the river, but is obstructed by rocks above and under water, over which the torrent rushes with great fury and noise, as may easily be conceived. The channel on the north side is now nearly dry, and is composed of great masses of slate with perpendicular fissures. The highest part of the island is 15 feet above the present level ; but from the marks on it the water in the rainy season must rise 12 feet, consequently covers the whole of the breadth of the channel, with the exception of the summit of the island ; and with the increased velocity must then produce a fall somewhat more consonant to the description of the natives. In ascending two hills we observed the river both above and below the fall to be obstructed by rocks as far as we could see, which might be a distance of about four miles. Highly disappointed in our expectations of seeing a grand cataract, and equally vexed at finding that the progress of the boats would be stopped, we climbed back to our people, whom we reached at four o'clock totally exhausted.

62. THE FATE OF TUCKEY'S EXPEDITION.

SIR R. F. BURTON.*

Of the fifty-four white men, eighteen, including eleven
of the *Congo* crew, died in less than three months. Fourteen
out of a party of thirty officers and men, who set out to
explore the cataracts *viâ* the northern bank, lost their
lives; and they were followed by four more on board
the *Congo*, and one at Bahia. The expedition remained
in the river between July 6 and October 18, little more
than three months; yet twenty-one, or nearly one-third,
three of the superior officers and all the scientific men,
perished. Captain Tuckey died of fatigue and exhaustion (October 4) rather than of disease; Lieutenant
Hawkey of fatal typhus (which during 1862 followed the
yellow fever, in the Bonny and New Calabar rivers); and
Mr. Eyre, palpably of bilious remittent. Professor Smith
had been so charmed with the river that he was with
difficulty persuaded to return. Prostrated four days afterwards by sickness on board the transport, he refused
physic and food, because his stomach rejected bark, and,
preferring cold water, he became delirious; apparently
he died of disappointment, popularly called a ' broken
heart.' . . .

The cause of this prodigious mortality appears in the
records of the expedition. Officers and men were all
raw, unseasoned, and unacclimatized. Captain Tuckey,
an able navigator, the author of ' Maritime Geography
and Statistics,' had served in the tropics; his biographer,
however, writes that a long imprisonment in France and
' residence in India had broken down his constitution,
and at the age of thirty (ob. æt. thirty-nine) his hair

* ' Two Trips to Gorilla Land.' (S. Low and Co., 1876.)

was grey and his head nearly bald.' The men perished,
exactly like the missionaries of old, by hard work, insufficient and innutritious food, physical exhaustion,
and by the doctor. At first 'immediate bleeding and
gentle cathartics' are found to be panaceas for mild
fevers; presently the surgeon makes a discovery as
follows: 'With regard to the treatment I shall here only
observe that bleeding was particularly unsuccessful.
Cathartics were of the greatest utility, and calomel, so
administered as speedily to induce copious salivation,
generally procured a remission of all the violent symptoms.' The phlebotomy was inherited from the mis-
sioners, who own almost to have blinded themselves by
it. When one was 'blooded' fifteen times and died, his
amateur Sangrado said, 'It had been better to have bled
him thirty times;' the theory was that in so hot a climate
all the European blood should be replaced by African.
One of the entries in Captain Tuckey's diary is: 'Awaking
extremely unwell, I directly swallowed five grains of
calomel.' A man worn out by work and sleeping in the
open air! The *Congo* sloop was moored in a reach surrounded by hills, instead of being anchored in mid-stream
where the current of water creates a current of air; those
left behind in her died of palm wine . . . and of exposure
to the sun by day and to the nightly dews. On the line
of march the unfortunate marines wore pigtails and
cocked hats, stocks and cross-belts, tight-fitting, short-
waisted red coats, and knee-breeches with boots or
spatter-dashes. Even the stout Lord Clyde in his latest
days used to recall the miseries of his march to Margate,
and declare that the horrid dress gave him more pain
than anything he afterwards endured in a lifetime of
marching. None seemed capable of calculating what
amount of fatigue and privation the European system

is able to support in the tropics.   And thus they perished,
sometimes of violent bilious remittents, more often of
utter weariness and starvation.

63. LIVINGSTONE'S DISCOVERY OF THE LUALABA.

SIR H. M. STANLEY, 1872.*

It is his firm belief that a man who rests his sole knowledge of the geography of Africa on theory deserves to
be discredited.   It has been the fear of being discredited
and criticised, and so made to appear before the world
as a man who spent so many valuable years in Africa for
the sake of burdening the geographical mind with theory,
that has detained him so long in Africa, doing his utmost
to test the value of the main theory which clung to him,
and would cling to him until he proved or disproved it.
This main theory is his belief that in the broad and
mighty Lualaba he has discovered the head waters of
the Nile.   His grounds for believing this are of such
nature and weight as to compel him to despise the warning that years are advancing on him, and his former
iron constitution is failing.   He believes his speculations
on this point will be verified; he believes he is strong
enough to pursue his explorations until he can return to
his country with the announcement that the Lualaba is
none other than the Nile.   On discovering that the in-
significant stream called the Chambezi, which rises
between 10° S. and 12° S., flowed westerly and then
northerly through several lakes, now under the names of
the Chambezi, then as the Luapula and then as the
Lualaba, and that it still continued its flow towards the
north for over 7°, Livingstone became firmly of the

* ' How I found Livingstone.'   (S. Low and Co., 1874.)

opinion that the river whose current he followed was the Egyptian Nile.   Failing at lat. 4° S. to pursue his explorations further without additional supplies, he determined to return to Ujiji to obtain them.

And now, having obtained them, he intends to return to the point where he left off work.   He means to follow that great river until it is firmly established what name shall eventually be given the noble waterway whose course he has followed through so many sick toilings and difficulties.   To all entreaties to come home and innumerable friends' offers he returns the determined answer : ' No ; not until my work is ended.'

64. THE LUALABA DISCOVERED TO BE THE CONGO.

CAPTAIN V. L. CAMERON,* 1874.

After two marches we came in sight of the mighty Lualaba.

From a bluff overhanging the river I obtained my first view of the stream—a strong and sweeping current of turbid yellow water fully a mile wide and flowing at the rate of three or four knots an hour, with many islands, much like the eyots on the Thames, lying in its course.

The larger ones were well wooded and inhabited by the Wagenya, a tribe holding all the islands and a long strip on the left bank, and as the sole proprietors of canoes, having the whole carrying trade of the river in their hands.

Canoes were numerous, and flocks of water - fowl, winging their way from sand - bank to sand - bank in search of food, gave life to the scene.   To remind us of the dangers of the stream there were enormous herds

* ' Across Africa.'   (G. Philip and Son.)

13—2

of hippopotami, blowing and snorting, and here and there the long scaly back of a crocodile floating almost flush with the water.

*　　*　　*　　*　　*

The levels I obtained at Nyangwé conclusively proved that the Lualaba could have no connection whatever with the Nile system, the river at Nyangwé being lower than the Nile at Gondokoro, below the point at which it has received all its affluents.

The volume of water also passing Nyangwé is 123,000 cubic feet per second in the dry season, or more than five times greater than that of the Nile at Gondokoro, which is 21,500 feet per second. This great stream must be one of the head-waters of the Kongo, for where else could that giant amongst rivers, second only to the Amazon in its volume, obtain the 2,000,000 cubic feet of water which it unceasingly pours each second into the Atlantic?

65. CAMERON CROSSES THE CONTINENT.*

1874.

Scrambling along a steep and rocky ridge of hills intersected by several watercourses and ravines with almost perpendicular sides, and then up a path not unlike a broken-down flight of steep steps, we reached the summit of the range.

What was that distant line upon the sky?

We all gazed at it with a strange mingling of hope and fear, scarcely daring to believe it was the sea. But looking more intently at that streak happily left no room for doubt.

It was the sea, and Xenophon and his ten thousand

* 'Across Africa.' (G. Philip and Son.)

could not have welcomed its view more heartily when they exclaimed, ' Θάλαττα! Θάλαττα !' than did I and my handful of way-worn followers.

There was little ' go ' left in me now. I was very nearly broken down ; for though my head and legs had ceased to ache so acutely, I was suffering excruciating pain in my back.

At almost every step I feared I should be compelled to lie down and wait for some assistance from the coast, but I thought of the poor exhausted fellows behind who were trusting to me to send them aid, and being sustained by the near approach of the end of my journey, I still managed to keep on my legs.

The remainder of this day was spent in crawling over rocks and dragging through pools, waist-deep, dammed up in hollows since the last rains, and now slimy and stagnant. I confess that it was a relief when, about four o'clock, I heard some of my men declare they could march no further ; for though I was fully aware of the vital importance of pushing on, and should have hesitated to suggest a halt, yet I was very weak and glad indeed to rest.

One of my people, and another of Manoel's being still able and ready to march, we despatched them with the letters I had recovered at Lungi, and a note, begging any charitably-disposed person to send a little food to meet us on the road. I then ate my last morsel of damper and turned in, intending the next day to make the final effort.

Somewhat refreshed by the night's rest, we continued our way through the pass until noon—the rays of the sun, reverberating from the rocks, making one feel as though in a furnace—and on emerging from it made our mid-day halt at an angle of the Supa, which drains the pass and falls into the sea at Katombéla.

On going to this stream to bathe, I was greatly surprised at my curious appearance, being covered with
purple spots; and I noticed that a slight bruise on my
ankle had developed into a large and angry-looking place.

I was still more astonished on lighting my pipe by
way of breakfast—for my pipe was now my only food—
to find my mouth bleeding. Of the cause I was ignorant,
for I did not then know that I was attacked with scurvy.

From some passing caravans we heard that our two
messengers had been seen that morning, and would by
this time have arrived at Katombéla.

On again, across a rough and waterless plain, lying
between us and the hills behind Katombéla and Benguella, and then over precipitous hills formed of limestone, with many huge ammonites and other fossils, and
having the appearance of cliffs which might once have
faced a sea. They were intersected by ravines and
dry watercourses, up and down the sides of which we
clambered in the dark, slipping about and bruising ourselves.

But what did it matter? The next morning would
see us at Katombéla.

At the bottom of a ravine we found water, which was
a godsend to me, for my mouth was still bleeding, and I
had already used that brought by us from our mid-day
halting-place.

Another steep climb brought us almost to the summit
of the last ridge, where it was somewhat level.

      *   *   *   *   *

One of my men, a short way in advance of me, now
shouted, ' Here's our camp-master ;' and, hastening on, I
saw Manoel's messenger.

He had with him a basket containing wine, bread, tins
of sardines, and a sausage ; and although my mouth

would not admit of my eating without pain, I managed to take some supper, for I had tasted nothing since the previous evening. From a note in English from Mr. Seruia, a trader at Katombéla who had kindly sent out these provisions, I learnt that my letters had been forwarded to Benguella. My messenger, it appeared, was too tired to return, so Mr. Seruia had sent one of his own people back with Manoel's man.

This was my last night outside the pale of civilization, and though thoroughly tired, I was much too excited to sleep.

Long before the rising of the sun we were all on the move, and, quickly finishing the remains of the supper, started on our last march. . . .

I found Katombéla situated on the seashore instead of ten or twelve miles inland, as I had imagined from the description given me.

A man engaged in searching for runaway slaves told me that rumours respecting an Englishman coming from the interior had been rife for some time, but no one had believed them.

I ran down the slope towards Katombéla, swinging my rifle round my head, which I believe was almost 'turned' for very joy; and the men, carried away with the same sense of relief, joined in the running till we approached nearer the town. Then I unfurled my colours and went forward more quietly.

Coming towards us I saw a couple of hammocks with awnings, followed by three men carrying baskets; and on meeting this party a jolly-looking little Frenchman jumped out, seized the baskets, and instantly opened a bottle to drink 'to the honour of the first European who had ever succeeded in crossing tropical Africa from east to west.'

66. DESCENT OF THE CONGO.

SIR H. M. STANLEY.* 1876-77.

From Mpungu we travelled through an interesting country (a distance of four miles), and suddenly from the crest of a low ridge saw the confluence of the Luama with the majestic Lualaba. The former appeared to have a breadth of 400 yards at the mouth; the latter was about 1,400 yards wide, a broad river of a pale grey colour, winding slowly from south and by east. . . . In the bed of the great river are two or three small islands, green with the verdure of trees and sedge. I likened it even here to the Mississippi, as it appears before the impetuous, full-volumed Missouri pours its rusty brown water into it.

A secret rapture filled my soul as I gazed upon the majestic stream. The great mystery that for all these centuries Nature had kept hidden away from the world of science was waiting to be solved. For 220 miles I had followed one of the sources of the Livingstone to the confluence, and now before me lay the superb river itself! My task was to follow it to the ocean.

*   *   *   *   *

Downward it flows to the unknown! to night-black clouds of mystery and fable, mayhap past the lands of the anthropoids, the pigmies, and the blanket-eared men of whom the gentle pagan king of Karagwé spoke, by leagues upon leagues of unexplored lands, populous with scores of tribes, of whom not a whisper has reached the people of other continents; perhaps that fabulous being the dread Macoco, of whom Bartolomeo Diaz, Cada Mosto, and Dapper have written, is still represented by one who inherits his ancient kingdom and power, and

* 'Through the Dark Continent.' (S. Low and Co.)

surrounded by barbarous pomp. Something strange
must surely lie in the vast space occupied by total
blankness on our maps between Nyangwé and 'Tuckey's
Farthest'!

*   *   *   *   *

Below Kaimba Island and its neighbour, the Livingstone assumes a breadth of 1,800 yards. The banks are
very populous; the villages of the left bank comprise
the district of Luavala. We thought for some time we
should be permitted to pass by quietly; but soon the
great wooden drums, hollowed out of huge trees, thundered
the signal along the river that there were strangers. In
order to lessen all chances of a rupture between us, we
sheered off to the middle of the river, and quietly lay on
our paddles. But from both banks at once, in fierce
concert, the natives, with their heads gaily feathered and
armed with broad black wooden shields and long spears,
dashed out towards us.

Tippu-Tib before our departure had hired to me two
young men of Ukusu—cannibals—as interpreters. These
were now instructed to cry out the word 'Sennenneh!'
('Peace!'), and to say that we were friends.

But they would not reply to our greeting, and in a
bold peremptory manner told us to return.

'But we are doing no harm, friends. It is the river
that takes us down, and the river will not stop, or go
back.'

'This is our river.'

'Good. Tell it to take us back, and we will go.'

'If you do not go back, we will fight you.'

'No, don't; we are friends.'

'We don't want you for our friends; we will eat you.'

But we persisted in talking to them, and, as their
curiosity was so great, they persisted in listening; and

the consequence was that the current conveyed us near
to the right bank, and in such near neighbourhood to
another district that our discourteous escort had to think
of themselves, and began to skurry hastily up river,
leaving us unattacked.

The villages on the right bank also maintained a
tremendous drumming and blowing of war-horns, and
their wild men hurried up with menace towards us,
urging their sharp-prowed canoes so swiftly that they
seemed to skim over the water like flying fish. Unlike
the Luavala villagers, they did not wait to be addressed ;
but as soon as they came within fifty or sixty yards they
shot out their spears, crying out, ' Meat ! meat ! Ah !
ha ! We shall have plenty of meat ! Bo-bo-bo-bo,
bo-bo-bo-bo-o-o !'

    *   *   *   *   *

It is the dread river itself of which we shall have now
to complain. It is no longer the stately stream whose
mystic beauty, noble grandeur, and gentle uninterrupted
flow along a course of nearly 900 miles ever fascinated
us, despite the savagery of its peopled shores; but a
furious river rushing down a steep bed obstructed by
reefs of lava, projected barriers of rock, lines of immense
boulders, winding in crooked course through deep chasms,
and dropping down over terraces in a long series of falls,
cataracts, and rapids. Our frequent contests with the
savages culminated in tragic struggles with the mighty
river as it rushed and roared through the deep yawning
pass that leads from the broad tableland down to the
Atlantic Ocean.

    *   *   *   *   *

After two miles we were abreast of the bay, or indenta-
tion, at which we had hoped to camp, but the strong

river mocked our efforts to gain it. The flood was
resolved we should taste the bitterness of death. A
sudden rumbling noise, like the deadened sound of an
earthquake, caused us to look below, and we saw the
river heaved bodily upward, as though a volcano was
about to belch around us. Up to the summit of this
watery mound we were impelled; and then, divining
what was about to take place, I shouted out, ' Pull, men,
for your lives!' A few frantic strokes drove us to the
lower side of the mound, and before it had finished subsiding, and had begun its usual fatal circling, we were
precipitated over a small fall, and sweeping down towards
the inlet into which the Nkenké Cataract tumbled, below
the lowest lines of breakers of the Lady Alice Rapids.
Once or twice we were flung scornfully aside and spun
around contemptuously, as though we were too insignifi-
cant to be wrecked ; then, availing ourselves of a calm
moment, we resumed our oars, and soon entering the
ebb-tide, rowed up river and reached the sandy beach at
the junction of the Nkenké with the Livingstone.

✷ ✷ ✷ ✷ ✷

Though our involuntary descent of the Lady Alice
Rapids from Gamfwé's Bay to Nkenké River Bay—a
distance of three miles—occupied us but fifteen minutes,
it was a work of four days, viz., from the thirteenth to
the sixteenth inclusive, to lower the canoes by cables.
Experience of the vast force of the flood, and the brittle-
ness of the rattan cables, had compelled us to fasten
eight cables to each canoe, and to detail five men to
each cable for the passage of the rapids. Yet, with all
our precautions, almost each hour was marked with its
special accident to man or canoe. One canoe, with a
man named Nubi in it, was torn from the hands of forty

men, swept down two miles, and sunk in the great whirlpool.

*   *   *   *   *

On the left side of the river I observed a line of rock-islets close to the shore. At the end of this long reach was a deep bend in the right bank, through which a lazy creek oozed slowly into the Livingstone. From this bend the great river ran south-south-west, and the roar of a great cataract two miles below became fearfully audible, and up from it light clouds of mist, and now and then spray showers, were thrown high into view. Towering above it, on the left, was the precipitous shoulder of a mountain ridge, the summit of which appeared crescent-shaped as we approached it from above. Picking our way towards it cautiously, close to projected reefy points, behind which are the entrances to the recesses in the mountainous bank already described, we arrived within fifty yards of the cataract of Isangila, or Tuckey's ' Second Sangalla.'

*   *   *   *   *

As the object of the journey had now been attained, and the great river of Livingstone had been connected with the Congo of Tuckey, I saw no reason to follow it farther, or to expend the little remaining vitality we possessed in toiling through the last four cataracts.

I announced, therefore, to the gallant but wearied Wangwana that we should abandon the river and strike overland for Embomma.

*   *   *   *   *

We had gradually descended some 500 feet along declining spurs when we saw a scattered string of hammocks appearing, and gleams of startling whiteness, such as were given by fine linen and twills.

A buzz of wonder ran along our column.

Proceeding a little farther we stopped, and in a short time I was face to face with four white—ay, truly white men!

As I looked into their faces, I blushed to find that I was wondering at their paleness. Poor pagan Africans— Rwoma of Uzinja and man-eating tribes of the Livingstone! The whole secret of their wonder and curiosity flashed upon me at once. What arrested the twanging bow and the deadly trigger of the cannibals? What but the weird pallor of myself and Frank! In the same manner the sight of the pale faces of the Embomma merchants gave me the slightest suspicion of an involuntary shiver. The pale colour, after so long gazing on rich black and richer bronze, had something of an unaccountable ghastliness. I could not divest myself of the feeling that they must be sick; yet, as I compare their complexions to what I now view, I should say they were olive, sunburnt, dark.

PART VII.

NORTH AFRICA.

INTRODUCTION.

Not much need be said by way of introduction to this part of our book, a necessary part, even if, as Mr. Grant Allen (see 67) points out, North Africa is properly to be considered as part of Europe. It has, for that very reason, been inhabited by nations who, unlike almost all the races of what we consider Africa proper, have played a great part in the world's history. A merely commercial Power establishes no great claim to the memory of posterity, still, it should be remembered that Carthage, of which few visible relics are left, was more than two thousand years ago one of the greatest commercial nations in the world; while Morocco, in much later times, rose to a height of culture which few countries in Europe at the same time could pretend to rival.

The extracts (68 and 70) from the Moorish historian and geographer known as Leo Africanus will show how widely the Morocco of his time, and much more that of a few centuries earlier still, differed from the Morocco of to-day. Parts of North Africa still are, as almost the whole of it until recently was, inaccessible to all but adventurous travellers; still, it has been the home of cultivated nations very much longer than those parts of Europe from which such travellers now generally come.

67. NORTH AFRICA REALLY A PART OF EUROPE.

GRANT ALLEN.*

NORTH AFRICA is an outlying fragment of Europe, which Mohammedan usurpation cut off for awhile from its natural surroundings, but which the expansion of the time is now bringing back once more with marvellous rapidity into full communion with its own proper and original continent.

The truth is, North Africa is not even by origin a part of the continent to which it has handed on its own much-abused name. The old Africa of the Mauritanian Afri has nothing at all to do with the new Africa of the barbarous negroes. It is, and has always been from the very beginning, an integral part of Europe, separated from Spain and Sicily only by the narrow seas at Gibraltar and Cape Bon, but divided from the great solid block of Negroland by the wide intervening expanse of the sandy desert. Egypt, in spite of its Mediterranean front, is a true portion of the Dark Continent, a mass of Nile mud deposited seaward by the endless river fed from the lakes and snowy mountains of the far interior. But Marocco, Algeria, Tunis, and in fact Tripoli, consist of a single long subsiding sierra of the Spanish system, artificially divided from the remainder of its mass by the accidental intrusion of the sea at Tangier and Carthage.

Whether the bed of Sahara was once an immense southern Mediterranean or not, it is at any rate certain that all the existing fauna and flora of the Atlas region—in which I will venture to include also the human inhabitants—entered the country from northward, from the

---

* ' A Glimpse of North Africa '—*Contemporary Review*, April, 1888.

European land area. The plants and animals are simply the plants and animals of Spain, Sicily, Italy, and Sardinia. The birds are just the larks and thrushes, the ortolans and plovers, that range over the greater part of Europe. The reptiles and insects are equally familiar in form and character. It is only in the extreme south, on the borders of the desert, that true African types like the panther and ostrich begin to appear as mere northward stragglers. A few fresh-water fish alone link the fauna of the Atlas to the African world; for the most part, Africa in the modern sense begins south of Sahara. Nevertheless, while in every physical and native characteristic the great bulge of land by the Syrtis and the Atlantic is all Europe, in external and artificial characteristics it must be frankly admitted that on the first flush it seems all Orient.

The visitor to Algiers, and far more to Tunis or Marocco, is struck at the outset, as he treads the Moorish shore, with an unwonted sense of novelty and foreignness. Everything at a first glance appears wonderfully unfamiliar. The tall and stately Arabs in their picturesque dirt; the melancholy Kabyles in their grimy burnouses; the flitting Moorish women, discreetly veiled with haik and yashmak up to their too loquacious eyes; the mosques and minarets, the domes and koubbas, the horseshoe arches, the Moslem architecture — all these seem to tell eloquently of something far from European or Christian. The very aspect of Nature is at the first glimpse equally fallacious. Date-palms and bananas in all the gardens give an almost tropical air to the squat and flat-roofed Moorish villas. Tall flowering aloes and prickly cactus hedges remind one instinctively at every turn of Mexico or Jamaica. Strings of laden camels, fresh in with dates or alfa-grass from the desert, and

14

negro traffickers from the oasis in gay-coloured robes,
increase the frequent suggestion of a Southern world.
Add to all these the gleaming, white-domed houses on
the dry red hillsides, and the tiled arcades of the white-
washed shrine where some holy marabout lies buried in
the odour of sanctity and the shade of the doum palms,
and you may be well excused for fancying yourself at
first really and truly in another continent.

But it is all show—mere external show—a shallow
veneering of Africa and Islam for all that. The country
was, and yet will be, Europe. The very things that
seemed so foreign at first sight are themselves as foreign
to the soil as to our observing eyes; they are all late
casual importations from warmer climates. The aloe
and the prickly pear come across the sea from the
American tropics; they grow in North Africa, as they
grow along the Riviera and on the Sicilian slopes, by
sufferance only. The further you get away from the
towns and civilization, the more do you leave whatever
seemed Africa behind you, and the more do you find
yourself frankly in Europe, except, of course, as regards
the human population. The dates and bananas and
agaves disappear, and you wander gradually into an
arid land of evergreen oak, and dry, healthy plants,
exactly like the barren white limestone hills about Mar-
seilles and Toulon. Almost every species of living thing
now found in the country on the Atlas slope has entered
it first from the northern shore—from Provence and
Spain—probably before the Straits of Gibraltar were
formed, and when land bridges existed viâ Sardinia and
Corsica on one side, or, again, viâ Reggio, Sicily, and
Cape Bon on the other. The few southern kinds are
every one of them recent immigrants or human importations. The camel is useless north of the Atlas; the

negro is an intruder. Land, plants, and animals, all alike, are purely European. . . .

For a time it was a question whether Africa or Italy, Carthage or Rome, was to rule the West ; and when Rome finally conquered, the completeness of her conquest and assimilation was more remarkable in Africa than even in Southern Gaul, in Spain, or in any other country outside Italy. It is surprising how firm a hold Roman civilization took upon all these rugged upland valleys. North Africa consists of an arid and crumbled mountain-chain, in whose tortuous recesses the French in Algeria have with difficulty planted a few outlying colonies, and maintained an often nominal and precarious supremacy. But Rome Romanized as well as conquered. Roman amphitheatres, baths, and temples of extreme magnificence, even far among the mountains, still stand as monuments to teach us how thoroughly the Italian had bent the Berber population to his own will. Aqueducts span half the gorges and ravines. Mosaics and inscriptions turn up by the dozen. Near Cherchel and Tipasa there are acres of sarcophagi. Nowhere in the world outside Italy, not even, I venture to say, in Provence itself, do Roman ruins and Roman remains strew the soil in such astonishing numbers as in Algeria and Tunis. Nowhere, too, did Christianity strike deeper root. Africa became the nursing-mother of saints and bishops, of martyrs and confessors, of schisms and heresiarchs. The country was apparently as Romanized as Cisalpine Gaul. Everywhere in the far interior Roman towns of striking size, adorned with triumphal arches, churches, palaces, and monuments, survive in fragments within their shrunken walls to bear witness to the great Catholic civilization which has passed away, for the time, from all North Africa. . . .

Well, the Arabs came and swept all this away. They divorced North Africa for twelve hundred years from its natural union with the opposite shore of the Mediterranean ; and they cut off the entire coast, from Egypt to Marocco, from intercourse with the civilized world of Europe. Ishmael's hand, here as elsewhere, was against every man. The Barbary pirates made civilization impossible at home and precarious on the Provençal and Ligurian seaboard. Of course there was a time when all this might have been otherwise; when it was doubtful whether Rome or Cordova was to become the centre of sweetness and light for the nations; whether Islam or Christendom was to evolve the philosophy and the science of the world. But when once that question was finally settled, North Africa fell back into a mere seething mass of anarchists and robbers. Christianity, commerce, art, science, all died down to the Mahommedan level. For twelve centuries this outlying fragment of the European world relapsed into a barbarism that grew deeper and deeper with each succeeding epoch. Islam formed an impenetrable barrier to the southward progress of civilizing ideas. All peaceable intercourse was wholly suspended. Africa seemed more readily accessible from the west, the south, or the east to European influences than from the old and natural highway of the north and the Mediterranean.

68. THE CITY OF MOROCCO IN 1525.

LEO AFRICANUS.*

This noble city of Morocco in Africa is accounted to be one of the greatest cities in the whole world. It is

* 'History and Description of Africa.' (Hakluyt Society, 1896.)

built upon a most large field, being about fourteen miles
distant from Atlas.

*   *   *   *   *

Here may you behold most stately and wonderful
workmanship, for all their buildings are so cunningly
and artificially contrived, that a man cannot easily
describe the same. This huge and mighty city, at
such time as it was governed by Hali, the son of King
Joseph, contained more than 100,000 families. It had
four-and-twenty gates belonging thereto, and a wall of
great strength and thickness, which was built of white
stone and lime. From this city the river of Tensift lieth
about six miles distant. Here may you behold great
abundance of temples, of colleges, of bath-stones, and of
inns, all framed after the fashion and custom of that
region. Some were built by the king of the tribe of
Luntuna, and others by Elmuachidin, his successor; but
the most curious and magnificent temple of all is that in
the midst of the city, which was built by Hali, the first
king of Morocco, and the son of Joseph aforesaid, being
commonly called the temple of Hali ben Joseph. Howbeit, one Abdul-Mumen which succeeded him, to the end
he might utterly abolish the name of Hali, and might
make himself only famous with posterity, caused this
stately temple of Morocco to be razed, and to be re-
edified somewhat more sumptuously than before. Howbeit, he lost not only his expenses, but failed of his purpose also; for the common people, even till this day,
do call the said temple by the first and ancientest
name.

Likewise in this city, not far from a certain rock, was
built a temple by him that was the second usurper over
the kingdom of Morocco, after whose death his nephew
Mansor enlarged the said temple fifty cubits on all sides,

and adorned the same with many pillars, which he commanded to be brought out of Spain for that purpose. Under this temple he made a cistern or vault as big as the temple itself; the roof of the said temple he covered with lead, and at every corner he made leaden pipes to convey rain-water into the cistern underneath the temple. The turret or steeple is built of most hard and well-framed stone, like unto Vespasian, his Amphitheatrum at Rome, containing in compass more than a hundred ells, and in height exceeding the steeple of Bononia. The stairs of the said turret or steeple are each of them nine handfuls in breadth, the utmost side of the wall is ten, and the thickness of the turret is five.

The said turret hath seven lofts, unto which the stairs ascending are very lightsome, for there are great store of windows, which, to the end they may give more light, are made broader within than without. Upon the top of this turret is built a certain spire or pinnacle, rising sharp in form of a sugar-loaf, and containing five-and-twenty ells in compass, but in height being not much more than two spears' length. The said spire hath three lofts, one above another, unto every of which they ascend with wooden ladders. Likewise, on the top of this spire standeth a golden half-moon, upon a bar of iron, with three spheres of gold under it, which golden spheres are so fastened unto the said iron bar that the greatest is lowest, and the least highest. It would make a man giddy to look down from the top of the turret, for men walking on the ground, be they never so tall, seem no bigger than a child of one year old. From hence, likewise, may you plainly descry the promontory of Azaphi, which notwithstanding is a hundred and thirty miles distant. But mountains, you will say, by reason of their huge bigness, may easily be seen afar off; howbeit, from this turret a man may in clear weather most easily see fifty miles into the plain countries.

The inner part of the said temple is not very beautiful; but the roof is most cunningly and artificially vaulted, the timbers being framed and set together with singular workmanship, so that I have not seen many fairer temples in all Italy. And albeit you shall hardly find any temple in the whole world greater than this, yet is it very meanly frequented, for the people do never assemble there, but only upon Fridays. Yea, a great part of this city, especially about the foresaid temple, lieth so desolate and void of inhabitants that a man cannot without great difficulty pass, by reason of the ruins of many houses lying in the way. Under the porch of this temple it is reported that in old time there were almost a hundred shops for sale of books, and as many on the other side over against them; but at this time I think there is not one bookseller in all the whole city to be found. And scarcely is the third part of this city inhabited.

69. MOROCCO TO-DAY.

JOSEPH THOMSON.[*]

For the first time we saw the Atlas before us in all its kingly elevation.

Hitherto we had only got glimpses of its higher peaks, but now the eye roamed from its dark bush and forest-clad base over its lower ranges to the snowy masses which broke through the grey fleecy clouds that here and there softly swathed its upper zones, and above them gleamed in dazzling whiteness against the blue sky, seemingly not of the gross earth at all. . . .

[*] 'Travels in the Atlas.' (G. Philip, 1889.)

From where we stood the range seemed to rise with extreme abruptness, dominating the plain with a frowning grandeur not noticeable on nearer approach, where the rise is seen to be more gradual and the central crest far indeed from overlooking the plain, or even its lower ranges. We could well have spent longer studying the physical features of this goal of our daydreams, but time was precious, and we turned to sweep our eyes over the great plain which lay between us and the mountains. There was but one feature to rivet our attention, and that was a great tower which rose from a dark mass of brown and green, like a lighthouse on a rock at sea. We did not require to be told that this was the tower or minaret of the Kutubia, the one striking monument which Southern Morocco possesses to tell of the former greatness of the empire and its present degeneracy. Around the Kutubia we had no difficulty in distinguishing the walls and houses, the gardens and date groves, that composed or encircled the city of Morocco. Of the plain itself little need be said. Bounded by the mountains, it seemed but a narrow strip of green and yellow, through which the River Tensift and its many tributaries meandered seaward, conspicuous lines of dark green in their shading of olive and date. Here and there dark patches told of fruit-yielding groves and of inhabitants, and Kubas showed where holy men were buried, though yet living to make intercession for those who believed. . . .

Our first impressions of the city of Morocco, this southern capital of a once glorious empire, were those of unmixed disappointment. As we wandered through street after street and lane after lane enclosed by clay-built walls and houses of meanest aspect, we saw much indeed of the ' havoc,' but very little of the ' splendour of

the East.' At every step we found evidence of a nation
on a down-grade slide, of a people who had lost all earthly
hopes and aspirations, and lived under the most grinding
oppression and tyranny. Morocco was a city grown
slattern, very much out at the elbows, and utterly care-
less of its personal appearance. And yet, as we per-
severed in our exploration, and got rid of our precon-
ceived notions, with all its air of dilapidation the city
again began to grow upon us. In the most unexpected
places, often midst tumbling ruins and all the signs of
rapid decay, we were continually attracted by a group of
palms or the sight of some interesting example of Moorish
workmanship.

Here it was a fountain on which the artist had lavished
all the wealth of his Oriental imagination, and shown all
his manipulative skill in stucco, wood-carving, tile-work,
and colour. There it was the horseshoe-shaped door-
way of a mosque overhung with effective mouldings.

We got delightful hasty glimpses of mosque interiors,
too, all the more attractive because forbidden and par-
taking of a spice of danger. These displayed cool aisles
and beautiful wall-decoration in stucco, arabesque, and
tile - work. There, in the subdued light, near the
Mihrab, pious Moslems could be seen prostrating themselves before the one God, and shady colonnades surrounded marble-paved courts, where sparkling fountains
cooled the air.

It was not, however, in its architectural features that
we found the special charm of Morocco. As in all
Oriental cities, it was its people and its street-scenes that
gave the most picturesque effects. The very beggars
carried their rags with such an air, they appealed to the
passer-by in such a high-flown and impressive style, that
they became not only objects of compassion, but subjects

for the artist. The women, swaddled in their absurd blanket-like coverings, carried about with them all the charm and mystery of the forbidden and the unseen. And yet not quite unseen either, for those beautiful eyes of theirs, sparkling with all their liquid brilliancy between black-tipped eyelids and long glossy eyelashes, transfix the gaze of the onlooker and fire his imagination, till he sees not only beautiful eyes, but face and form, and all the other allurements of the sex to match. Not least attractive were the substantial city men of Morocco mounted on quick-pacing mules, or the Government officials on gorgeously caparisoned and prancing barbs; while the weather-beaten Berbers from the Atlas, the gaunt, fierce-eyed Arabs from Sus and the desert, and the shrinking, money-grabbing Jew, all formed effective elements in the scene.

It was in the purely business parts of the town, however, that we found most to admire. Motley throngs of buyers and sellers, busy workmen and idle wayfarers, crowded the narrow thoroughfares, and, with the quaint box-like shops on either side, formed an exhaustless vista of picturesque scenes.

70. FEZ IN 1525.

LEO AFRICANUS.[*]

A world it is to see, how large, how populous, how well fortified and walled this city is. The most part thereof standeth upon great and little hills, neither is there any plain ground, but only in the midst of the city. The river entereth the town in two places, for it is divided into a double branch, one whereof runneth by new Fez—that

[*] 'History of Africa.' (Hakluyt Society.)

is, by the south side of the town—and another cometh
in at the west side. And so almost infinitely dispersing
itself into the city, it is derived by certain conducts and
channels unto every temple, college, inn, hospital, and
almost to every private house. Unto the temples are
certain square conducts adjoined, having cells and
receptacles round about them, each one of which hath
a cock, whereby water is conveyed through the wall into
a trough of marble, from whence flowing into the sinks
and gutters, it carrieth away all the filth of the city into
the river. In the midst of each square conduct standeth
a low cistern, being three cubits in depth, four in breadth,
and twelve in length, and the water is conveyed by
certain pipes into the foresaid square conducts, which
are almost a hundred and fifty in number.

The most part of the houses are built of fine bricks
and stones curiously painted. Likewise their bay-
windows and portals are made of parti-coloured brick,
like unto the stones of Majorica. The roofs of their
houses they adorn with gold, azure, and other excellent
colours, which roofs are made of wood, and plain on the
top, to the end that in summer-time carpets may be
spread upon them, for here they use to lodge by reason
of the exceeding heat of that country. Some houses are
of two and some of three stories high, whereunto they
make fine stairs, by which they pass from one room to
another under the same roof, for the middle part of the
house is always open or uncovered, having some chambers
built on the one side, and some on the other. The
chamber-doors are very high and wide, which in rich
men's houses are framed of excellent and carved wood.
Each chamber hath a press, curiously painted and var-
nished, belonging thereunto, being as long as the chamber
itself is broad ; some will have it very high, and others

but six handfuls in height, that they may set it on the
tester of a bed.

All the portals of their houses are supported with brick
pillars finely plastered over, except some which stand
upon pillars of marble. The beams and transoms up-
holding their chambers are most curiously painted and
carved. To some houses likewise belong certain square
cisterns, containing in breadth six or seven cubits, in
length ten or twelve, and in height but six or seven
handfuls, being all uncovered, and built of bricks trimly
plastered over. Along the sides of these cisterns are
certain cocks, which convey the water into marble
troughs, as I have seen in many places of Europe.
When the foresaid conducts are full of water, that which
floweth over runneth by certain secret pipes and convey-
ances into the cisterns, and that which overfloweth the
cisterns is carried likewise by other passages into the
common sinks and gutters, and so into the river. The
said cisterns are always kept sweet and clean, neither
are they covered but only in summer-time, when men,
women, and children bathe themselves therein.

     *   *   *   *   *

Moreover, in the city of Fez are two most stately
colleges, of which divers rooms are adorned with curious
painting; all their beams are carved, their walls consisting both of marble and freestone. Some colleges there
are which contain a hundred studies, some more, and
some fewer, all which were built by divers kings of the
Marin family. One there is among the rest most beautiful and admirable to behold, which was erected by a
certain king called Habu Henon. Here is to be seen an
excellent fountain of marble, the cistern whereof con-
taineth two pipes. Through this college runneth a little
stream in a most clear and pleasant channel, the brims

and edges whereof are workmanly framed of marble, and stones of Majorica.

Likewise, here are three cloisters to walk in, most curiously and artificially made, with certain eight-square pillars of divers colours to support them. And between pillar and pillar the arches are beautifully overcast with gold, azure, and divers other colours, and the roof is very artificially built of wood. The sides of these cloisters are so close that they which are without cannot see such as walk within. The walls round about, as high as a man can reach, are adorned with plaster-work of Majorica. In many places you may find certain verses, which declare what year the college was built in, together with many epigrams in the founder's commendation, the letters of which verses are very great and black, so that they may be read afar off. This college gates are of brass, most curiously carved, and so are the doors artificially made of wood.

In the chapel of this college standeth a certain pulpit, mounted nine stairs high, which stairs are of ivory and ebony. Some affirm that the king, having built this college, was desirous to know how much money he had spent in building it ; but after he had perused a leaf or two of his account-book, finding the sum of forty thousand ducats, he rent it asunder, and threw it into the foresaid little river, adding this sentence out of a certain Arabian writer : ' Each precious and amiable thing, though it costeth dear, yet, if it be beautiful, it cannot choose but be good cheap ; neither is anything of too high a price which pleaseth a man's affection.'

71. FEZ AT THE PRESENT TIME.

W. B. HARRIS,* 1889.

Fez—Fas it is called by the Moors—is the capital, or
northern capital, of Morocco, and is by far the most
important town in the Empire, not only on account of
its size and the number of its residents, but also as being
one of the official residences of the Sultan and Court, and
on account of its trade.

Certainly no town in the country boasts such a situation
as Fez. The city of Morocco is as picturesquely, or
even more picturesquely, situated; but whereas the latter
owes more to its surroundings, the former is in itself
superior in position, for the town lies on the slopes of the
Wad Fas, a small, fast-running stream, an affluent of
the Sebou, and is thus, both as regards health and our
ideas of situation, far more advantageously placed. The
two capitals have much alike, however; in fact there is
much that pertains equally to all Moorish cities—the
total want of restoration, or even repair, the dirt, the
smells, and the rough, muddy or stony roads, full of
holes leading into what little drainage there is; but
perhaps these holes are there on purpose to point out
to the traveller the fact that drains do exist. This I
know, that though two years separated my visits to Fez,
yet I remembered the holes, and took special guard to
keep my horse out of them when riding through the
streets for the second time; and there they were, a little
larger, perhaps, from the number of horses, mules, and
donkeys that must in that period have stepped into them,
and perhaps broken a leg or two.

The history of Fez is composed of wars and murders,

* 'Land of an African Sultan.' (S. Low and Co.)

triumphs of arts and sciences, and a good deal of imagination.

Even the founding of Fez is a matter of doubt; but authorities seem to agree in giving 800 A.D. as about the probable date.

     *   *   *   *   *

From that time till some two centuries ago it increased rapidly, became a seat of learning to which even Spaniards were sent to finish their education, where astronomy was to some extent understood, where medicine was progressing in rapid strides, and where poets were putting upon their vellum scrolls, and in vellum books, the old songs of Spain. How things are changed now! The roofs have fallen from the colonnades of the colleges and mosques; astronomy has given place to the lowest ideas of astrology; medicine is but the concoction of a filthy potion, or a few words scrawled on a small piece of paper and worn round the neck; vellum is unknown, and they use kitchen-paper instead; poetry has disappeared. . . .

Yet Fez is a charming old city. After all, it is only as if we let Cambridge fall a little more to ruin, give time to the statues on Caius gate to gain respectability by age, and to allow the grass to grow in full luxuriance over the John's and Trinity tennis-courts. We should love Cambridge just the same then, I think, perhaps more; and I am sure I should prefer the wicked, idle Fez of to-day to the bustling Fez of two or three centuries ago. There is not a great deal remaining in the Fez of to-day to tell of these brighter and happier times, but two mosques of great beauty still stand almost intact— those of the Kairouin, and the sacred shrine of Moulai Idrees.

The former is probably by far the largest mosque in

North Africa, and what glimpses we were able to obtain of its interior did not belie Leo and Rohlfs, both of whom rave about its magnificence.   Row after row of columns and arches, dusky colonnades, only half-lighted by the coloured lamps that hang suspended from the roof, a great sunlit court full of worshippers, two exquisite erections of tall, graceful columns with carved roofs shading a marble fountain-basin with its ever-gurgling water ; such is the mosque of the Kairouin.

By passing a small side-gate we were several times able for some minutes at a time to stand and gaze upon the impressive scene, to watch the long line of worshippers prostrate themselves and rise again at the voice of one who read the Koran in a particularly nasal accent.   This mosque boasts a fine minaret, from which the muezzin calls to prayer at the appointed hours.

PART VIII.

MISCELLANEOUS.

INTRODUCTION.

A FEW words may be said here by way of preface to the last section of this book, designed to convey some idea, however faint, of the variety of the strange customs and strange creatures which are, or have been, to be seen by the African explorer. If some things are recorded, as the story of the peaceable lions in 80, which it may well be doubted whether anyone ever did or ever will see, we must not forget that it has taken a very long acquaintance with the world to make man even as competent as he is now to decide upon what is probable; also that many strange African stories have turned out to have much more truth in them than was at one time thought likely. The legends of the Pygmies (see 87) cannot well be less than 3,000 years old, for Homer had heard of the little people who, as it was supposed, had to fight the cranes when they flew southwards in the winter. Yet though many rumours of their existence have reached Europe, both in ancient and modern times (see 37, 60, 75), it was not attested nor generally believed in until the latter half of the present century. Perhaps they had a much wider range in ancient times, before the encroachments of stronger races drove them to the recesses

15

of the forests in which Andrew Battel (see 75) heard of them, and Sir H. M. Stanley saw them.

It took a long time to persuade people to believe in the gorilla, which Andrew Battel was the first to introduce to the modern world by the name of Pongo. It is not quite so formidable an animal as Battel's informants believed, but we know, even now, very little about its habits. Battel's second monster, the Engeco, can be easily identified, for this word, which is now spelt, more scientifically, ' nschego ' or 'ndjeko,' is still one of the native names for the chimpanzee.

The endeavours of Ptolemy Philadelphus (see 85) to stop the persecution of the African elephant were so far from successful that Bruce, some two thousand years later, found the perilous method of overcoming the elephant by hamstringing him with a sharp sword still practised in the same part of Africa. It must, indeed, have been a sport far surpassing in excitement even the modern rifle-shooting, which is working a much wider destruction. It is an extremely curious thing that the ancients were certainly able to domesticate the African elephant, which the moderns, apparently, can only massacre.

---

72. GENERAL DESCRIPTION OF AFRICA.

PROFESSOR H. DRUMMOND.*

Africa, speaking generally, is a vast, ill-formed triangle. It has no peninsulas ; it has almost no islands or bays or fjords. But three great inlets, three mighty rivers piercing it to the very heart, have been allocated by a kind Nature one to each of its solid sides. On the north is the river of the past, flowing through Egypt, as Leigh

* ' Tropical Africa.'   (Hodder and Stoughton, 1888.)

Hunt says, 'like some grave, mighty thought threading a dream;' on the west the river of the future, the not less mysterious Congo; and on the east the little-known Zambesi.

The physical features of this great continent are easily grasped. From the coast a low scorched plain, reeking with malaria, extends inland in unbroken monotony for two or three hundred miles. This is succeeded by mountains slowly rising into a plateau some 2,000 or 3,000 feet high; and this, at some hundreds of miles' distance, forms the pedestal for a second plateau as high again. This last plateau, 4,000 to 5,000 feet high, may be said to occupy the whole of Central Africa. It is only on the large scale, however, that these are to be reckoned plateaux at all. When one is upon them he sees nothing but mountains and valleys and plains of the ordinary type, covered for the most part with forest.

I have said that Nature has supplied each side of Africa with one great river. By going some hundreds of miles southward along the coast from Zanzibar the traveller reaches the mouth of the Zambesi. Livingstone sailed up this river once, and about 100 miles from its mouth discovered another river twisting away northwards among the mountains. The great explorer was not the man to lose such a chance of penetrating the interior. He followed this river up, and after many wanderings found himself on the shores of a mighty lake. The river is named the Shiré, and the lake—the existence of which was quite unknown before—is Lake Nyassa. Lake Nyassa is 350 miles long, so that with the Zambesi, the Shiré, and this great lake, we have the one thing required to open up East Central Africa—a water-route to the interior.

But this is not all. Two hundred and fifty miles from

the end of Lake Nyassa, another lake of still nobler proportions takes up the thread of communication. Lake
Tanganyika is 450 miles in length. Between the lakes
stands a lofty plateau, cool, healthy, accessible, and
without any physical barrier to interrupt the explorer's
march. By this route the Victoria Nyanza and the
Albert Nyanza may be approached with less fatigue,
less risk, and not less speed, than by the overland trail
from Zanzibar. At one point also along this line, one is
within a short march of that other great route which
must ever be regarded as the trunk-line of the African
continent. The watershed of the *Congo* lies on this
Nyassa-Tanganyika plateau. This is the stupendous
natural highway on which so much of the future of East
Central Africa must yet depend.

73. AFRICAN FEVER.

WINWOOD READE.*

Next to sea-sickness fever is perhaps the most facetious
of diseases; it always comes on like a practical joke.
A. B. on a certain evening is in unusually high spirits.
His imagination is active; he feels inclined to exercise
his brain, and begins to write a long letter home, saying,
among other things, that he has not had the fever yet,
and does not think he will.

But somehow he finds it difficult to settle down to his
task for any length of time. Conversation is more to his
humour; he becomes excited in the course of it, drinks
a little, goes to bed, sleeps with difficulty, has a series of
dreams, and awakes feeling anything but well. He does
not eat much breakfast, but thoroughly enjoys his cup

* 'The African Sketch-Book.' (Smith, Elder and Co., 1873.)

of tae. At twelve o'clock he is seated with his friends in the piazza, suffering like themselves from the intense heat. Presently he puts on his coat. He gives a shudder; he becomes pale; his features shrink; his hair bristles up; his nails turn blue. He is taken off to bed; blankets are piled upon him, hot-water bottles are applied to his feet, warm drinks are poured down his throat; but the bed shakes with his shiverings, and his teeth chatter so loudly that they can be heard across the room. He is transported to the Arctic regions. Suddenly he is whisked back to Africa, and then from Africa into the hottest room of the hottest Turkish bath that ever was invented. The cold stage is over, and the hot stage has begun. Putting your hand on his forehead is like putting it on a stove. Often delirium intervenes. There is always an agonizing thirst, which should be freely indulged with fresh lemonade or with cold water, if nothing else is to be had.

Then comes the grateful stage of resolution. The pores at length open, and shed an abundant and refreshing rain on the surface of the skin. The paroxysm is over, and the patient feels himself weak, but otherwise as well as before. Let us suppose that he does not *cut* the fever, as it is called. The next day passes; the feebleness about the knee-joints is departing; he believes that he has nothing more to fear. On the day after that he is again in the piazza; it is again the sultry hour of noon. He is again imbibing his favourite beverage and smoking his cigar, and again comes that mysterious shudder; again he is alternately iced and roasted, like the souls in Dante's 'Inferno'; and so on indefinitely, unless the usual medicine be administered—viz., Peruvian bark in the compact form of sulphate of quinine.

74. THE TSETSE-FLY.

J. CHAPMAN.[*]

A word with regard to that insignificant-looking insect, the Tsetse, or Poison-fly. This great barrier to African travelling was first met by the Boers and other travellers on the Limpopo, and though most people on their first encounters felt doubts regarding its repute of the sting being fatal to horses and cattle, too painful experience of its ravages has left no doubt on the subject. We find, again, the insect rising here, after we have completed more than a thousand miles of our explorations towards the unknown interior of Central Africa, crossing our path and stopping our progress in every direction.

The tsetse is, in extreme length, half an inch, or very little more, and has very much the appearance of a young bee just escaped from its cell, or a bee half drowned in honey, the wings being always closed when stationary. The body is not quite so long as that of a bee, and much more slender. It is marked with alternate stripes of yellow and dark chestnut in transverse bands on the back of the abdomen, which, fading towards the centre of the back, gives it the appearance of having a longitudinal stroke of yellow immediately down the vertebra, the belly livid-white, glossy, dusky-brown wings, folding over each other, eyes purple, six long legs, and its proboscis from one-sixth to one-eighth of an inch long. It has tufts of hair over the body, which are longest at the mouth, on the back of the thorax, which is brown with black spots, and at the extremity of the abdomen. It is extremely quick of sight, and keen of scent; its flight is rapid and straight.

The bite of the tsetse is something like that of the

[*] 'Travels in South Africa.' (Stanford, 1868.)

mosquito, but the pain not so lasting. It assails different animals in their most defenceless parts : a man behind the back between the shoulders, and an ox on the back or under the belly ; a horse in the same places, and inside the nostrils; and a dog on the forehead, etc. With the proboscis they penetrate a pilot cloth coat and whole suit of under-clothes. The bite of this insect is fatal to cattle, horses, sheep, and dogs ; but there is a peculiar breed of the latter known as *makoba* dogs, which are exempt from the effects of its poison, the breed having from time immemorial been reared in the ' fly ' country, and escaped a *cow-milk diet*, as the natives say. It has no ill-effects whatever on game or upon men, except that the being bitten by numbers is likely to induce head-ache, as with the irritation of mosquitoes.

The symptoms, as I have observed them, are, first, in the ox, a swelling under the throat, which, if lanced, emits a yellowish fluid. The hair stands on end, or is reversed. The animals become debilitated ; and, though the herbage be ever so luxuriant, refuse to eat their fill, and become thin. The eyes water, and at length, when the end is approaching, a continual rattling in the throat may be heard at a few paces' distance. It sometimes happens that a fly-bitten ox will live, but very rarely, and only when it has no work to perform. Work and rain are great precipitators of their end. In horses the symptoms are swelling about the eyes and nostrils, the hair is reversed, and, though they have the best of food, they become thin, sleepy, and, pining gradually, at length die.

Both cattle and horses live from fourteen days to six months after having been bitten by tsetse, but they generally die after the first rain has fallen. A dog dies in ten or twelve days, or two or three weeks at latest.

It is perceptible in the eyes, which are swollen and pro-truding. After death the heart of an ox is generally incased in a yellowish glutinous substance, which might be mistaken for fat. The flesh is full of little bladders of fluid, and the blood also is half fluid, which becomes con-gealed on cooling. The vitals are of a livid colour. The tsetse fly is generally found within a few miles of water, in rich, sandy ridges near marshy spots, and generally in mopani or mimosa forests. I have known them to shift their positions, or encroach on new ground, or leave parts where firearms have driven the game out of a district.

They are mostly only found within a certain range from water. To the buffalo in particular the insect is more attached, and often moves about with them in the rainy season. The thorax of the tsetse is brown, covered with hairs, and is divided into *three* sections, by two transverse indentations across the middle, the posterior or triangular one having a white margin like the tail of a soldier's coat, being edged with dull white, and a stripe down the middle. The middle section has four oblique oblong, dark spots, and the front section one or two irregular spots. These markings are, however, very capricious, perhaps differing in male and female.

75. ANDREW BATTEL'S ADVENTURES.*

1603.

About this time news was brought by some Jesuits that the Queen of England was dead, and that King James had made peace with Spain. On which I pre-sented a petition to the governor, who consented I should return to my native country; as he and his train were going to the city of St. Paul, I went with them.

* Pinkerton's ' Voyages,' 1814.

The governor left 500 soldiers in the fort of Cambamba, which they still hold. I then went with a Portuguese merchant to the province of Bamba, and from thence to the Onteiro or city, standing on a mountain of Congo; from thence to Gongon and Balta, where we sold our commodities, and after an absence of six months returned to the city again; from whence I purposed to have taken ship for Spain, and from thence home to England. But the governor retracted his word, and ordered me to be ready in two days to go on another expedition to Auyoykayongo. As this governor had served his three years, and another was expected every day, I determined to absent myself till the new governor's arrival, and then return, as every new governor on his arrival makes proclamation for all deserters and others to return with free pardon.

That night I left the city with two negro boys I had, who carried my musket, five pounds of powder, a hundred bullets, and what little store of provision I could collect. By the morning I had got about twenty miles from the city, by the side of the River Bengo. Here I stayed some days, and then passed the river, and came to the River Dande, lying to the northward on the way to St. Paul, with the intention of hearing news from thence, for which purpose I sent one of my negroes to inquire of those who passed about the new governor, who brought me word to a certainty that the new governor should not come this year. I was now put to my shifts, whether I would return to the city and be hanged, for I had run away twice, or conceal myself in the woods. I determined on the latter, and lived in that manner a month, between the Rivers Dande and Bengo. I then went again to Bengo, to Mani Kaswea, passed over the river, and went to the lake of Casanza, about which is the

greatest quantity of wild beasts in any part of Angola.
Near this lake I stayed six months, living upon dried
flesh, such as deer, roebucks, etc., which I killed with
my musket, and dried the flesh as the savages do upon
a hurdle 3 feet from the ground, making underneath a
great fire, and laying upon the flesh green boughs which
keep the smoke and heat of the fire down and dry it. I
made my fire with two little sticks as the savages do.
Sometimes my negro boys procured me some Guinea
wheat from the inhabitants, in exchange for pieces of
dried fish. The lake of Casanza abounds with fish of
various sorts. I have taken up a fish called somb, which
skipped out of the water on shore, four feet long. Thus,
after having lived six months on dried fish and flesh,
and seeing no likelihood of an end to my sufferings, I
endeavoured to hit upon some means of getting away.

In this lake are many islands full of trees called membre,
which are as light and as soft as cork. Of these trees, by
the help of a knife I had of the savages, I made a Jergado
in the fashion of a boat, nailed it with wooden pegs, and
railed it all round to prevent the sea washing me out,
and with a blanket I had I made a sail ; I likewise made
three oars for rowing. Thus equipped, my two negroes
and I ventured ourselves upon the lake, which is eight
miles over, and rowed to the River Bengo, and going
down twelve leagues with the current to the bar, which
is dangerous to pass, owing to the roughness of the sea ;
but having passed it safely, rowed into the sea, and sailed
along the coast, which I was very well acquainted with,
intending to go to the kingdom of Longo lying to the
north. Passing the night at sea, next day I saw a pinnace
sailing before the wind from the city. When we came
close together I found the master of her to be one of my
old friends and messmates. He was bound to San Thome,

and out of friendship took me in, and set me on shore at the port of Longo, where I remained three years, and got into great favour with the king, owing to my killing him deer and wild-fowl with my gun.

* * * * *

The province of Mayombo is so overgrown with wood that one may travel twenty days in the shade without being the least incommoded by sun or heat. They have no tillage or grain of any sort, nor any kind of tame cattle or fowls, the people living on the flesh of elephants, which they very much esteem, and other wild beasts; plantains, a great variety of roots, which are very good, and nuts; they are well supplied with fish. Two leagues to the southward of Cape Negro, which is the port of Mayombo, is a large sandy bay. Sometimes the Portuguese lade logwood in this bay; into it runs a large navigable river named Banna, the navigation of which is sometimes impeded by a bar. In it are many inhabited islands. The woods are so infested with baboons, monkeys, apes, and parrots, that it is dangerous to venture alone among them. Here are also two kinds of monsters common to those woods. The largest of them is called Pongo in their language, and the other Engeco. The Pongo is in all his proportions like a man (except the legs, which have no calves), but are of a gigantic size. Their faces, hands, and ears are without hair. Their bodies are covered, but not very thick, with hair of a dunnish colour. When they walk on the ground it is upright, with their hands on the nape of the neck. They sleep in trees and make a covering over their heads to shelter them from the rain; they eat no flesh, but feed on nuts and other fruits. They cannot speak, nor have they any understanding beyond instinct.

When the people of the country travel through the

woods, they make fires in the night, and in the morning
when they are gone, the Pongos will come and sit round
it till it goes out, for they do not possess sagacity enough
to lay more wood on.   They go in bodies, and kill many
negroes who travel in the woods.   When elephants happen
to come and feed where they are, they will fall on them,
and so beat them with their clubbed fists and sticks that
they are forced to run away roaring.   The grown Pongos
are never taken alive, owing to their strength, which is
so great that ten men cannot hold one of them.   The
young Pongos hang upon their mother's belly, with their
hands clasped about her.   Many of the young ones are
taken by means of shooting the mothers with poisoned
arrows, and the young ones, hanging to their mothers,
are easily taken.

       *   *   * .   *   *

There is another lord towards the east who is called
Mani Kesoch; he resides eight days' journey from
Mayombo. . . .

To the north-east of Mani Kesoch are a kind of little
people called Matimbas, who are no bigger than boys
twelve years old; but are very thick, and live only upon
flesh, which they kill in the woods with their bows and
darts.   They pay tribute to Mani Kesoch, and bring all
their elephants' teeth and tails to him.   They do not
enter the houses of the Marambas, nor suffer them to
come where they dwell.   And if by chance a Maramba,
or people of Longo, pass where they dwell, they forsake
that place and go to another.   The women carry bows
and arrows as well as the men, and walk single in the
woods to kill the Pongos with their poisoned arrows.

76. THE GREAT FOREST OF CENTRAL AFRICA.

SIR H. M. STANLEY, 1888.*

For 160 days we marched through the forest, bush, and jungle without ever having seen a bit of greensward of the size of a cottage chamber floor. Nothing but miles and miles, endless miles of forest, in various stages of growth and various degrees of altitude, according to the ages of the trees, with varying thickness of undergrowth, according to the character of the trees, which afforded thicker or slighter shade.

*　　　*　　　*　　　*　　　*

It is an absolutely unknown region opened to the gaze and knowledge of civilized man for the first time since the waters disappeared and were gathered into the seas, and the earth became dry land.

*　　　*　　　*　　　*　　　*

Imagine the whole of France and the Iberian peninsula closely packed with trees varying from 20 to 180 feet high, whose crowns of foliage interlace and prevent any view of sky and sun, and each tree from a few inches to 4 feet in diameter. Then from tree to tree run cables from 2 inches to 15 inches in diameter, up and down in loops and festoons and W's and badly-formed M's; fold them round the trees in great tight coils, until they have run up the entire height, like endless anacondas. Let them flower and leaf luxuriantly, and mix up above with the foliage of the trees to hide the sun; then from the highest branches let fall the ends of the cables reaching near to the ground by hundreds with frayed extremities, for these represent the air-roots of the Epiphytes. Let

* 'Through Darkest Africa.' (S. Low and Co.)

slender cords hang down also in tassels with open thread-
work at the ends. Work others through and through
these as confusedly as possible, and pendent from branch
to branch, with absolute disregard of material, and at
every fork and on every horizontal branch plant cabbage-
like lichens of the largest kind, and broad spear-leaved
plants—these would represent the elephant-eared plant—
and orchids and clusters of vegetable marvels, and a
drapery of delicate ferns, which abound.

Now cover tree, branch, twig, and creeper with a thick
moss like a green fur. Where the forest is compact, as
described above, we may not do more than cover the
ground closely with a thick crop of phrynia and amoma
and dwarf bush; but if the lightning, as frequently
happens, has severed the crown of a proud tree, and let
in the sunlight, or split a giant down to its roots, or
scorched it dead, or a tornado has been uprooting a few
trees, then the race for air and light has caused a multitude
of baby trees to rush upward—crowded, crushing, and
treading upon and strangling one another, until the whole
is one impervious bush.

＊   ＊   ＊   ＊   ＊

To complete the mental picture of this ruthless forest,
the ground should be strewn thickly with half-formed
humus of rotting twigs, leaves, branches; every few
yards there should be a prostrate giant, a reeking compost
of rotten fibres and departed generations of insects and
colonies of ants, half veiled with masses of vines and
shrouded by the leafage of a multitude of baby saplings,
lengthy briars, and calamus in many fathom lengths;
and every mile or so there should be muddy streams,
stagnant creeks, and shallow pools, green with duck-
weed; leaves of lotus and lilies, and a greasy green
scum composed of millions of finite growths.   Then

people this vast region of woods with numberless fragments of tribes who are at war with each other, and who
live apart from ten to fifty miles in the midst of a prostrate forest, amongst whose ruins they have planted the
plantain, banana, manioc, beans, tobacco, colocassia,
gourds, melons, etc., and who, in order to make their
villages inaccessible, have resorted to every means of
defence suggested to wild men by the nature of their
lives. They have planted skewers along their paths,
and cunningly hidden them under an apparently stray
leaf, or on the lee side of a log, by striding over which
the naked foot is pierced, and the intruder is either killed
from the poison smeared on the tops of the skewers, or
lamed for months. They have piled up branches, and
have formed abattis of great trees, and they lie in wait
behind with sheaves of poisoned arrows, wooden spears,
hardened in fire, and smeared with poison.

*   *   *   *   *

We were bitten and stung by pismires and numberless
tribes of insects by day, which, everyone will confess, is
as bad as being whipped with nettles; the night had also
its alarms, terrors, and anxieties. In the dead of night,
when the entire caravan was wrapped in slumber, a
series of explosions would wake everyone. Some tree
or another was nightly struck by lightning, and there
was a danger that half the camp might be mangled by
the fall of one; the sound of the branches during a storm
was like the roar of breakers, or the rolling of a surge on
the shore. When the rain fell, no voice could be heard
in the camp; it was like a cataract with its din of falling
waters. Each night, almost, a dead tree fell with startling crackle, and rending and rushing, ending with the
sound which shook the earth.

There were trees parting with a decayed member, and

the fall of it made the forest echo with its crash as
though it were a fusillade of musketry. The night winds
swayed the branches, and hurled them against each other
amid a chorus of creaking stems, and swinging cables
and rustle of leaves. Then there was the never-failing
crick of the cricket, and the shriller but not less monotonous piping call of the cicadæ, and the perpetual chorus
of frogs ; there was the doleful cry of the lemur to his
mate—a harsh, rasping cry which made night hideous,
and loneliness and darkness repulsive. There was a
chimpanzee at solitary exercise, amusing himself with
striking upon a tree like the little boys at home rattle a
stick against the area railings. There were the midnight
troops of elephants, who, no doubt, were only prevented
from marching right over us by the scores of fires scattered
about the camp.

77. THE WHITE ANT.

PROFESSOR H. DRUMMOND.*

It is a small insect, with a bloated, yellowish-white
body, and a somewhat large thorax, oblong-shaped, and
coloured a disagreeable oily brown. The flabby, tallow-
like body makes this insect sufficiently repulsive, but it
is for quite another reason that the white ant is the
worst abused of all living vermin in warm countries.

The termite lives almost exclusively upon wood, and
the moment a tree is cut, or a log sawn for any economical
purpose, this insect is upon its track. One may never
see the insect, possibly, in the flesh, for it lives underground; but its ravages confront one at every turn.
You build your house, perhaps, and for a few months

* ' Tropical Africa.' (Hodder and Stoughton, 1888.)

fancy you have pitched upon the one solitary site in the country where there are no white ants. But one day suddenly the door-post totters, and lintel and rafters come down together with a crash. You look at a section of the wrecked timbers, and discover that the whole inside is eaten clean away. The apparently solid logs of which the rest of the house is built are now mere cylinders of bark, and through the thickest of them you could push your little finger. Furniture, tables, chairs, chests of drawers, everything made of wood, is inevitably attacked, and in a single night a strong trunk is often riddled through and through, and turned into match-wood. There is no limit, in fact, to the depredation by these insects, and they will eat books, or leather, or cloth, or anything; and in many parts of Africa, I believe if a man lay down to sleep with a wooden leg it would be a heap of sawdust in the morning.

*   *   *   *   *

The material excavated from these underground galleries and from the succession of domed chambers—used as nurseries or granaries—to which they lead, has to be thrown out upon the surface. And it is from these materials that the huge ant-hills are reared, which form so distinctive a feature of the African landscape.

These heaps and mounds are so conspicuous that they may be seen for miles, and so numerous are they, and so useful as cover to the sportsman, that without them in certain districts hunting would be impossible. The first things, indeed, to strike the traveller in entering the interior are the mounds of the white ant, now dotting the plain in groups like a small cemetery, now rising into mounds, singly or in clusters, each 30 or 40 feet in diameter, and 10 or 15 feet in height; or, again, standing out against the sky like obelisks, their bare sides carved

16

and fluted into all sorts of fantastic shapes. In India these ant-heaps seldom attain a height of more than a couple of feet, but in Central Africa they form veritable hills, and contain many tons of earth.

The brick houses of the Scotch mission-station on Lake Nyassa have all been built out of a single ants' nest, and the quarry from which the material has been derived forms a pit beside the settlement some dozen feet in depth. A supply of bricks, as large again, could probably still be taken from this convenient depôt; and the missionaries on Lake Tanganyika and onwards to Victoria Nyanza have been similarly indebted to the labours of the termites. In South Africa the Zulus and Kaffirs pave all their huts with white ant earth; and during the Boer War our troops in Pretoria, by scooping out the interior from the smaller beehive-shaped ant-heaps, and covering the top with clay, constantly used them as ovens.

78. LOCUSTS.

THOMAS SHAW,* 1725.

I never observed the mantes to be gregarious; but the locusts, properly so-called, which are so frequently mentioned by sacred as well as profane writers, are sometimes so beyond expression. Those which I saw, *ann.* 1724 and 1725, were much bigger than our common grasshoppers, and had brown spotted wings, with legs and bodies of a bright yellow. Their first appearance was towards the latter end of March, the wind having been for some time from the south. In the middle of April their numbers were so vastly increased, that in the heat of the day they formed themselves into large and

* Pinkerton's 'Voyages,' 1814.

numerous swarms, flew in the air like a succession of clouds, and, as the prophet Joel (ii. 10) expresses it, they *darkened the sun*. When the wind blew briskly, so that these swarms were crowded by others, or thrown one upon another, we had a lively idea of that comparison of the psalmist (Ps. cix. 23) of being *tossed up and down as the locust*.

In the month of May, when the ovaries of those insects were ripe and turgid, each of these swarms began gradually to disappear, and retired into the Mettijiah and other adjacent plains, where they deposited their eggs. These were no sooner hatched in June than each of the broods collected itself into a compact body of a furlong or more in square; and marching afterwards directly forward towards the sea, they let nothing escape them, eating up everything that was green and juicy; not only the lesser kind of vegetables, but the vine likewise, the fig-tree, the pomegranate, the palm, and the apple-tree— *even all the trees of the field* (Joel i. 12). In doing which *they kept their ranks like men of war*, climbing over, as they advanced, every tree or wall that was in their way; nay, they entered into our very houses and bed-chambers like *so many thieves*.

The inhabitants, to stop their progress, made a variety of pits and trenches all over their fields and gardens, which they filled with water; or else they heaped up therein heath, stubble, and such-like combustible matter, which were severally set on fire upon the approach of the locusts. But this was all to no purpose, for the trenches were quickly filled up, and the fires extinguished by infinite swarms succeeding one another; whilst the front was regardless of danger, and the rear pressed on so close, that a retreat was altogether impossible. A day or two after one of these broods was in motion, others were already hatched to march and glean after them, gnawing off the very bark and the young branches of such trees as had before escaped with the loss only of their fruit and foliage. So justly have they been compared by the prophet Joel (ii. 3) to *a great army*, who further observes that *the land is as the garden of Eden before them, and behind them a desolate wilderness.*

Having lived near a month in this manner, like a μυριοστομον ξιφος, or *sword with ten thousand edges,* to which they have been compared, upon the ruin and destruction of every vegetable substance that came in their way, they arrived at their full growth, and threw off their nympha-state by casting their outward skin. To prepare themselves for this change, they clung by their hinder feet to some bush, twig, or corner of a stone, and immediately, by using an undulating motion, their heads would first break out, and then the rest of their bodies. The whole transformation was performed in seven or eight minutes, after which they lay for a small time in a torpid and seemingly in a languishing condition; but as soon as the sun and the air had hardened their wings by drying up the moisture that remained upon them after casting their sloughs, they re-assumed their former voracity, with an addition both of strength and agility. Yet they continued not long in this state before they were entirely dispersed, as their parents were before, after they had laid their eggs; and as the direction of the marches and flights of them both was always to the northward, and not having strength, as they have sometimes had, to reach the opposite shores of Italy, France, or Spain, it is probable they perished in the sea, a grave which, according to these people, they have in common with other winged creatures.

79. THE LION'S ROAR.

COLONEL GORDON CUMMING.*

The night of the 19th was to me rather a memorable one, as being the first on which I had the satisfaction of hearing the deep-toned thunder of the lion's roar. Although there was no one near to inform me by what beast the haughty and impressive sounds which echoed through the wilderness were produced, I had little difficulty in divining. There was no mistake about it ; and on hearing it I at once knew, as well as if accustomed to the sound from my infancy, that the appalling roar which was uttered within half a mile of me was no other than that of the mighty and terrible king of beasts.

  ✻   ✻   ✻   ✻   ✻

One of the most striking things in connection with the lion is his voice, which is extremely grand and peculiarly striking. It consists at times of a low, deep moaning, repeated five or six times, ending in faintly audible sighs. At other times he startles the forest with loud, deep-toned, solemn roars, repeated five or six times in quick succession, each increasing in loudness to the third or fourth, when his voice dies away in five or six low, muffled sounds, very much resembling distant thunder. At times, and not unfrequently, a troop may be heard roaring in concert, one assuming the lead, and two, three, or four more regularly taking up their parts, like persons singing a catch. Like our Scottish stags at certain seasons, they roar loudest in cold, frosty nights ; but on no occasions are their voices to be heard in such perfection, or so intensely powerful as when two or three strange troops of lions approach a fountain to drink at

* ' Five Years of a Hunter's Life.' (Murray, 1850.)

the same time. When this occurs every member of each troop sounds a bold roar of defiance at the opposite parties; and when one roars, all roar together, and each 'seems to vie with his comrades in the intensity and power of his voice. The power and grandeur of these nocturnal forest concerts is inconceivably striking and pleasing to the hunter's ear. The effect, I may remark, is greatly enhanced when the hearer happens to be situated in the depths of the forest, at the dead hour of midnight, unaccompanied by any attendant, and ensconced within twenty yards of the fountain which the surrounding troops of lions are approaching. . . .

As a general rule lions roar during the night, their sighing moans commencing as the shades of evening envelop the forest, and continuing at intervals throughout the night. In distant and secluded regions, however, I have constantly heard them roaring loudly as late as nine and ten o'clock on a bright sunny morning. In hazy and rainy weather they are to be heard at every hour in the day, but their roar is subdued. It often happens that when two strange male lions meet at a fountain a terrific combat ensues, which not unfrequently ends in the death of one of them. The habits of the lion are strictly nocturnal; during the day he lies concealed beneath the shade of some low bushy tree or wide-spreading bush, either in the level forest or on the mountain-side. He is also partial to lofty reeds, or fields of long rank yellow grass, such as occur in low-lying vleys. From these haunts he sallies forth when the sun goes down, and commences his nightly prowl. When he is successful in his beat, and has secured his prey, he does not roar much that night, only uttering occasionally a few low moans, that is, provided no intruders approach him, otherwise the case would be very different. Lions are ever most active, daring, and presuming in dark and stormy nights ; and consequently on such occasions the traveller ought more particularly to be on his guard. I remarked a fact connected with the lions' hour of drinking peculiar to themselves : they seemed unwilling to visit the fountains with good moonlight. Thus, when the moon rose early, the lions deferred their hour of watering until late in the morning ; and when the moon rose late, they drank at a very early hour in the night. . . .

Owing to the tawny colour of the coat with which Nature has robed him he is perfectly invisible in the dark, and although I have often heard them loudly lapping the water under my very nose, not twenty yards from me, I could not possibly make out so much as the outline of their forms. When a thirsty lion comes to water he stretches out his massive arms, lies down on his breast to drink, and makes a loud lapping noise in drinking, not to be mistaken. He continues lapping up the water for a long while, and four or five times during the proceeding he pauses for half a minute as if to take breath. One thing conspicuous about them is their eyes, which, in a dark night, glow like two balls of fire.

80. A STRANGE LION STORY.

CAPTAIN V. L. CAMERON.*

I heard many curious stories which, although they may seem to be 'travellers' tales,' were vouched for by independent witnesses, and, I am convinced, thoroughly believed in by those who recounted them.

Amongst these narratives the palm may perhaps be

* 'Across Africa.' (G. Philip and Son.)

given to one related by a native of Ukaranga. He asserted that in the village next to that in which he lived the people were on most friendly terms with the lions, which used to walk in and about the village without attempting to injure anyone. On great occasions they were treated to honey, goats, sheep and ugali, and sometimes at these afternoon drums as many as 200 lions assembled. Each lion was known to the people by name, and to these they responded when called. And when one died the inhabitants of the village mourned for him as for one of themselves..

This village was reported to be situated on the shores of Lake Tanganyika, not very distant from Jumah Merikani's house; and he also told me that this friendship between the natives and lions was commonly spoken of, but he had never been present at one of the gatherings. The Mkaranga, however, asserted that he had often witnessed this friendly intercourse between man and beast, and brought several of his tribesmen to testify to the truth of his statement.

Certainly, if this be true, our most famous lion-tamers have yet something to learn from the natives of Africa.

Another story had a curious resemblance to that of the upas-tree. At a certain place in Urguru, a division of Unyamwési, are three large trees with dark-green foliage, the leaves being broad and smooth. A travelling-party of Warori, on seeing them, thought how excellent a shelter they would afford, and camped under them; but the next morning all were dead, and to this day their skeletons and the ivory they were carrying are said to remain there to attest their sad fate.

Jumah assured me he had seen these trees, and that no birds ever roosted on their branches, neither does any grass grow under their deadly shade; and some men who were with him when he passed them corroborated his statement in every particular.

He also told me that in the vicinity of Mfuto, a town near Taborah, figures of a man seated on a stool, with his drum, dog, and goat, were carved in the solid rock; and Arabs had informed him that in the Uvinza to the east of Tanganyika there was a large well with carved and perfect arches.

This work was ascribed by the natives to a former race of Wasungu, but the Arabs supposed it to have been executed by Suliman ibn Daood and the genii.

81. THE AFRICAN PALM-WINE.

M. ADANSON.*

The oily palm is of all others that which shoots to the greatest height. Here are some from 60 to 80 feet in the stalk, without any branches. The trunk is outwardly black, equally large through the whole length of it, and from 1 to 2 feet in diameter. Its head is loaded with leaves pretty much like the date-tree. It bears a round fruit the size of a small nut, and covered with a yellow pulp, of which they make the palm-oil. The negroes call it *tir*.

It is from these two trees they extract the palm-wine, which is exactly the colour of whey. There are several methods of extracting it; the first, practised by the negroes, and which I have often followed after their example in regard to the date-tree of the forest of Krampsane, is this: they cut a stalk a few inches under the crown, and leave only some leaves standing; then they lay the leaves above the incision and fasten them

* ' A Voyage to Senegal,' 1759.

with a peg to the tree. The extremity of those leaves is
folded afterwards into a calabash, or into a small earthen
pot, narrow-mouthed, and suspended so as not to quit
the leaves, or to fall. By this method the sap which
issues from the stalk distils along the leaves, and is
collected together in the earthen pot.

The second method of extracting the palm-wine consists in making a round hole under the head of the tree
instead of cutting it, and in introducing into this hole a
few folded leaves, which serve as a gutter or passage to
convey the liquor into the pot or vessel fastened to it.

These two methods are easy to practise in regard to
the date-tree, as they only make an incision in the stalk,
which is not above five feet high. But when they are
obliged to extract the wine from a very tall tree, as from
the oily palm, there is a great deal more difficulty in the
operation. The negroes have an admirable way of doing
it. They take a girth of the bark of *bauhinia*, or of the
leaves of a palmetto-tree, dried in the sun, beaten and
twisted, the breadth of thrice the thickness of one's
finger. At one end they make an eyelet-hole, into which
they put a little stick, fastened across the other end, to
serve as a button. This girth must be neither too pliant
nor too stiff, but should have a sufficient elasticity to
hinder it from giving way too much. It makes a sort
of circle of $2\frac{1}{2}$ feet in diameter, and when stretched by
the man's body and the tree, it becomes an oval, leaving
the distance of $1\frac{1}{2}$ feet between both. With this girth
they tie themselves, as it were, to the oily palm, and
climb up at first with their feet, then working with their
hands and knees till the part of the girth fastened to the
tree becomes lower than that which supports their reins
and thighs, and serves them as a seat to rest upon; then
they draw near the tree in order to raise the opposite

end, which is soon after brought down below the part that sustains their reins, which have been raised by working with the feet and knees. The girth cannot slip, because it is always very tight between the man and the trunk, and the latter is, moreover, very rough. In this manner they soon get to the top; there they sit on their girth, and, enjoying the liberty of their arms, they first cut the bottom of those fruits which they think are ripe; then fastening them to calabashes, they fill these with wine, and let them down by a cord; for they never for-·get, in going up, to carry with them a bandoleer, containing everything requisite for this kind of work, such as a cord, a knife, and empty calabashes, to supply the place of those which they have filled with liquor. When they want to come down, they go a contrary way to work to what they did in climbing up; that is, they lower the girth from time to time instead of raising it. Their quickness and resolution in this toilsome task show plainly how supple and dextrous they must be, for it is never mentioned that any accident has happened them; and they have nothing to fear but the breaking of the girth.

This kind of vintage must cost the negroes very little trouble, since their wine is so cheap that you have above forty pints upon the spot for ten sous, and very often for half that price. It is not all made at the same time, according to the custom of making wine of the juice of the grape in temperate countries. The trees furnish daily but a small quantity of this liquor, and they are obliged to consume it directly, because it soon grows sour. The negroes do not drink it till twenty-four hours after it is drawn, that is, till it has fermented enough to stimulate the palate agreeably. It is drinkable till the third day, but then it grows heady, and there is danger in being intoxicated with it. After that time it turns into bad vinegar, which soon contracts an abominable smell.

82. GRASS-BURNING.

J. BRUCE,* 1768.

This soil, called by the Abyssinians *Mazaga*, when wet by the tropical rains, and dissolving into mire, forces these savages to seek for winter quarters. Their tents under the trees being no longer tenable, they retire with their respective foods, all dried in the sun, into caves dug into the heart of the mountains, which are not in this country basaltes, marble, or alabaster, as is all that ridge which runs down into Egypt along the side of the Red Sea; but are of a soft, gritty, sandy stone, easily excavated and formed into different apartments. Into these, made generally in the steepest part of the mountain, do these savages retire to shun the rains, living upon the flesh they have already prepared in the fair weather.

I cannot give over the account of the Shangalla without delivering them again out of their caves, because this return includes the history of an operation never heard of, perhaps, in Europe, and by which considerable light is thrown upon ancient history. No sooner does the sun pass the zenith, going southward, than the rains instantly cease; and the thick canopy of clouds, which had obscured the sky during their continuance, being removed, the sun appears in a beautiful sky of pale blue, dappled with small thin clouds, which soon after disappear, and leave the heavens of a most beautiful azure. A very few days of the intense heat then dries the ground so perfectly that it gapes in chasms; the grass, struck at the roots

* 'Travels to Discover the Source of the Nile.'

by the rays, supports itself no more, but droops and becomes parched. To clear this away, the Shangalla set fire to it, which runs with incredible violence the whole breadth of Africa, passing under the trees, and following the dry grass among the branches with such velocity as not to hurt the trees, but to occasion every leaf to fall.

*   *   *   *   *

While what I have said is still in memory, I must apply a part of it to explain a passage in Hanno's 'Periplus.' We saw, says that bold navigator, when rowing close along the coast of Africa, rivers of fire, which ran down from the highest mountains, and poured themselves into the sea ; this alarmed him so much that he ordered his galleys to keep a considerable offing.

After the fire has consumed all the dry grass on the plain, and, from it, done the same up to the top of the highest mountain, the large ravines or gullies, made by the torrents falling from the higher ground, being shaded by their depth, and their being in possession of the last water that runs, are the latest to take fire, though full of every sort of herbage. The large bamboos, hollow canes, and such-like plants, growing as thick as they can stand, retain their greenness, and are not dried enough for burning till the fire has cleared the grass from all the rest of the country. At last, when no other fuel remains, the herdsmen on the top of the mountains set fire to these ; and the fire runs down in the very path in which, some months before, the water ran, filling the whole gully with flame, which does not end till it is checked by the ocean below where the torrent of water entered, and where the fuel of course ceases. This I have often seen myself, and been often nearly inclosed in it ; and can bear witness that, at a distance, and by a stranger ignorant of the cause, it would very hardly be distinguished from a river of fire.

83. LAKE TANGANYIKA.

SIR R. F. BURTON,* 1858.

On the 13th February, 1858, we resumed our travel through screens of lofty grass, which thinned out into a straggling forest. After about an hour's march, as we entered a small savannah, I saw the Fundi before alluded to running forward and changing the direction of the caravan. Without supposing that he had taken upon himself this responsibility, I followed him. Presently he breasted a steep and stony hill, sparsely clad with thorny trees; it was the death of my companion's riding-ass. Arrived with toil—for our fagged beasts now refused to proceed—we halted for a few minutes upon the summit. ' What is that streak of light which lies below ?' I inquired of Seedy Bombay. ' I am of opinion,' quoth Bombay, ' that this is *the* water.' I gazed in dismay; the remains of my blindness, the veil of trees, and a broad ray of sunshine illuminating but one reach of the lake, had shrunk its fair proportions. Somewhat prematurely I began to lament my folly in having risked life and lost health for so poor a prize, to curse Arab exaggeration, and to propose an immediate return, with the view of exploring the Nyanza or Northern Lake. Advancing, however, a few yards, the whole scene suddenly burst upon my view, filling me with admiration, wonder, and delight.

* * * * *

Nothing, in sooth, could be more picturesque than this first view of the Tanganyika Lake, as it lay in the lap of

* ' The Lake Regions of Central Africa.' (Longmans, 1860.)

the mountains, basking in the gorgeous tropical sunshine.
Below and beyond a short foreground of rugged and
precipitous hill-fold, down which the foot-path zigzags
painfully, a narrow strip of emerald green, never sere
and marvellously fertile, shelves towards a ribbon of
glistening yellow sand, here bordered by sedgy rushes,
there cleanly and clearly cut by the breaking wavelets.
Further in front stretch the waters, an expanse of the
lightest and softest blue, in breadth varying from thirty
to thirty-five miles, and sprinkled by the crisp east wind
with tiny crescents of snowy foam. The background in
front is a high and broken wall of steel-coloured mountain ; here flecked and capped with pearly mist, there
standing sharply pencilled against the azure air, its
yawning chasms, marked by a deeper plum-colour, fall
towards dwarf hills of mound-like proportions, which
apparently dip their feet in the wave. To the south,
and opposite the long low point, behind which the Mala-
garazi river discharges the red loam suspended in its
violent stream, lie the bluff headlands and capes of
Uguhha, and, as the eye dilates, it falls upon a cluster
of outlying islets, speckling a sea-horizon.

Villages, cultivated lands, the frequent canoes of the
fishermen on the waters, and on a nearer approach the
murmurs of the waves breaking upon the shore, give a
something of variety, of movement, of life to the landscape,
which, like all the fairest prospects in these regions, wants
but a little of the neatness and finish of art—mosques
and kiosks, palaces and villas, gardens and orchards—
contrasting with the profuse lavishness and magnificence
of nature, and diversifying the unbroken *coup-d'œil* of
excessive vegetation, to rival, if not to excel, the most
admired scenery of the classic regions.

The riant shores of this vast crevasse appeared doubly

beautiful to me after the silent and spectral mangrove-
creeks on the East-African seaboard, and the melancholy,
monotonous experience of desert and jungle scenery,
tawny rock, and sun-parched plain or rank herbage and
flats of black mire. Truly it was a revel for soul and
sight! Forgetting toils, dangers, and the doubtfulness
of return, I felt willing to endure double what I had
endured, and all the party seemed to join with me in
joy.

84. KILIMANJARO.

JOSEPH THOMSON.*

At the very outset let me confess that I shrink from
the task of attempting to convey any idea of this colossal
mountain. I feel that the subject is beyond the power
of my puny pen, and that here, after all, I am very much
on a level with the untutored Masai savage, who simply
stands awe-struck before the sublime spectacle, and tells
you it is the ' Ngajé Ngai,' or House of God.

The term Kilima-Njaro has generally been understood
to mean the Mountain (Kilima) of Greatness (Njaro).
This probably is as good a derivation as any other,
though not improbably it may really mean the ' White '
mountain, as I believe the term ' Njaro ' has in former
times been used to denote whiteness.

*   *   *   *   *

Kilimanjaro, in its horizontal and vertical extension,
may be described as a great, irregular, pear-shaped mass,
with its major axis in a line running north-west and
south-east, the tapering point running into the heart of
the Masai country. On this line it is nearly sixty miles
long. Its minor axis, running at right angles, reaches

* ' Through Masai Land ' (S. Low and Co., 1885.)

only to some thirty miles. As we have already had
occasion to remark, the mountain is divided into the
great central mass of Kibo, and the lower conical peak
of Kimawenzi. Towards the north-west it shades away
into a long ridge, which gradually tapers horizontally
and vertically till it becomes merged in the Masai Plain.

The southern aspect of this stupendous mountain
(which Von der Decken by triangulation has ascertained
to be little short of 19,000 feet at its highest point on
Kibo) forms the country of Chaga, which may be
described as a great platform, basement, or terrace,
from which the dome and peak abruptly rise. This
platform may be described as rising from 4,000 to 6,000
feet, over ten miles of rounded ridges, and characterized
by deep glens at its broadest part. The features of this
region, though in themselves rich and pleasing in the
extreme, and presenting a smiling aspect with variegated
plantations, yet somewhat detract from the imposing
grandeur of the mountain, as the eye has to wander a
distance of more than fifteen miles, before Kibo, at a
height of some 12,000 feet, springs precipitously heaven-
ward.

The features of the lower aspect are disappointingly
even and monotonous. You look in vain for rugged
rocks, or overhanging precipices, for striking angulari-
ties, or for inequalities in the shape of peaks or other
excrescences. Rounded outlines everywhere meet the
gaze. There is nothing savage. There are no striking
effects of light and shade ; a dull monotone rules both in
form and colour. The scene is entirely suggestive of
solidity and repose, of serene majesty asleep. The finest
effects, indeed, are to be seen when great cumulus clouds
tumble and roll across the face of the mountains, now
closing in the scene, anon breaking up and whirled into

17

fragments, throwing a checkered shade over the moun-
tain-slopes. Such is the aspect of the mountain across
the greater part of Chaga. Towards the great western
ridge, however, the scene is more striking, for here the
clear sweep of the mountain may be seen unbroken from
top to bottom.

*   *   *   *   *

It is from the north side, however, that the grandest
view of the whole mountain can be obtained. Standing
a short distance off on the great Njiri Plain, we see
the entire mountain, horizontally and vertically, without
moving the head. Rising from the almost level sandy
plain at an altitude of about 3,000 feet, it springs at an
even angle to a sheer height of 15,000 feet, unbroken by
a single irregularity or projecting buttress. No cones or
hills diversify its surface. Neither gorge nor valley cuts
deep into its sides. You see on your left the great cone
of Kimawenzi, with only one or two slight indentations
sweeping round in a saddle-shaped depression to spring up
into a dome of the most perfect proportions, curving over
as if projected by an architect's hand rather than that of
Nature, which abhors unbroken lines.

The snow-cap shows here to great advantage, forming
a close-fitted, glittering helmet, artistically laid on the
massive head of Kibo, and at times looking not unlike
the aureole, as represented in many old pictures of saints,
as it scintillates with dazzling effect under the tropical
sun. The resemblance to an aureole is made all the
more complete by the manner in which long tongues or
lines of snow extend down the mountain-side, filling up
a series of seams or flutings, formed, doubtless, by the
erosive action of the melting snow, which, going on
incessantly, counterbalances the continuous fall. Here,
still more than on the south side, is Kilimanjaro lacking

in the picturesque. You are not startled or bewildered by a multiplicity of detail. The magnificent mass only suggests a divine repose and grandeur.

*   *   *   *   *

Nature, indeed, seems to consider this spectacle too sacred to be always seen, and keeps it, as a rule, enveloped in soft gray mists and stratus clouds. Occasionally its godlike presence is revealed as it greets the dawning sun and bathes in the rich hues and crimson glows of its early rays, to be immediately after hidden by a weird, ghost-like haze, which, suddenly springing up no larger than the hand, spreads with remarkable rapidity till nothing but a blank expanse of gray meets the gaze. And yet the scene does not always close thus, for not uncommonly the upper part of Kibo is descried away up in mid-heaven, cut off apparently from all earthly connection, shining clear and bright with dazzling effulgence, suggesting a sight of the very heavens opened, a marvel of whiteness, and most fitting emblem of ethereal purity. This certainly is the most striking spectacle presented by Kilimanjaro. As seen projected against the upper sky like a mirage, it gives the spectator the notion of stupendous height, and, as I have already said, all that he can whisper to himself is the awe-struck words of the Masai warrior, ' Ngajé Ngai !' (The House of God).

85. ANCIENT ELEPHANT-HUNTING.

AGATHARCHIDES,* ABOUT B.C. 115.

Agatharchides says that the Ptolemy who reigned next after the son of Lagos [i.e. Ptolemy Philadelphus] was the first to organize the hunting of elephants and other

* From the abstracts in Photius and Diodorus Siculus, book iii.

17—2

equally wild animals, and of set design to bring together in one region what Nature had placed far apart. . . .

The Ethiopian hunters who attack the elephant dwell at a considerable distance to the west [of the river Atbara]. Living in a region of thickets and dense woods, they watch, by keeping a look-out in the tallest trees, for the places where the elephants go in, and where they turn aside to rest. The herds they never attack, deeming such an attempt hopeless, but on solitary elephants they venture with a strange audacity to lay hands. When the animal is on the right hand, as viewed from the tree in which the watcher may be hiding, then in the moment of its passing he grasps its tail with his hands, while with his feet he plants himself upon its left thigh. He is provided with an axe slung to his shoulders, light as required for the delivery of a one-handed stroke, but extraordinarily sharp, with which, grasping it in his right hand, he severs the tendon of the right ham, dealing repeated blows, while, with the left hand, he keeps his body in position. The inconceivable quickness with which they perform this feat is due to the consideration that in every case the man's life is at stake ; he must subdue the animal or die, the circumstances admitting no other alternative. It sometimes happens that the beast thus hamstrung, unable by its natural clumsiness to twist round, but swaying towards the injured part, falls and involves the Ethiopian in its destruction. Sometimes, too, it crushes the man against a rock or tree, and by the weight of its body squeezes him to death. But other elephants, in the agony of their wounds, far from seeking to defend themselves against their assailant, take to flight over the plain, until the striker, by dint of bringing down his axe constantly on the same spot, cuts through the tendons and paralyses the animal. On its fall they run up in throngs, and begin their feast by hacking the flesh from its hinder parts while it is yet alive.

There are, however, neighbouring tribes who, overcoming strength by art, hunt the elephant without risk to themselves. For it is the habit of this animal, when satiated with feeding, to betake itself to sleep in a manner unlike all other quadrupeds. Not being able to let down the whole weight of its body to the ground by bending its knees, it takes its repose in sleep while leaning against a tree. Consequently the tree, owing to this repeated contact, becomes worn and soiled; the ground, too, surrounding it displays footprints and many tokens by which the Ethiopians, who are looking out for them, discover the elephants' sleeping-places. And as often as they happen upon such a tree, they saw it through close to the ground, till it needs only a slight pressure to make it fall; then, after removing the traces of their presence, they decamp before the animal arrives on the scene. The elephant, having eaten his fill, returns to his accustomed sleeping-place; but directly he leans with all his weight upon the tree, he bears it down and is borne with it to the ground. Here he lies, a feast prepared ready for the hunters, who, cutting into the hinder parts of the animal, bleed it to death. They encamp upon the spot, and remain there until they have consumed their fallen prey.

And Agatharchides says that Ptolemy, the King of Egypt, exhorted these hunters to give over the slaughter of the elephants that he might obtain them alive; but, though he made them many handsome offers, he not only failed to persuade them, but received from them the reply that they would not exchange their present manner of life for his whole kingdom.

86. THE HONEY-GUIDE.

MAJOR SERPA PINTO.[*]

No sooner does man penetrate into one of the extensive forests of South Central Africa than the *indicator*
makes its appearance, hopping from bough to bough in
close proximity to the adventurer, and endeavouring by
its monotonous note to attract his attention. This end
having been attained, it rises heavily upon the wing, and
perches a little distance off, watching to see if it is
followed.

If no attention be paid to it, it again returns, hopping
and chirping as before, and, by its conduct and the
manner of its flight, evidently invites the stranger to
follow in its wake. The wayfarer yields at length,
moved by the pertinacity of the bird, which, now flying,
now hopping, but so as never to get out of sight of its
follower, guides him through the intricacies of the forest,
almost unerringly, to a bees' nest.

This is the most common instance, and the aborigines,
who are hunting after wax, invariably allow themselves
to be guided by its indications.

Some explorers, and among them the Portuguese
Gamito, declare that the bird likewise entices men on
to the den of the wild beast. This I cannot endorse of
my own experience, as I have followed dozens of *indi-
cators*, nor did I ever hear it affirmed by any native.

True, this restless bird has guided me and others to
the carcass of some animal wasting in putrefaction, to
an encampment recently abandoned, to a lake, or to
other wayfarers; but why it should do any of these
things is a mystery, inasmuch as it is in nowise a gainer

[*] ' How I crossed Africa.' (S. Low and Co., 1881.)

by such a proceeding. But the fact remains that it shows man almost always the way to honey, and I believe it to be its fixed intention so to do; although, if the other destinations to which I have alluded, and which have produced the impression made upon many travellers, have been reached upon the road, it can scarcely be deemed remarkable in African forests.

For the same reason, it is very possible that a lion's den may stand in the way without its being the bird's intention to entice the traveller into the beast's jaws.

Admitting, however, that the general rule that the *indicator* points the road to where honey may be found has exceptions, the examples of the rule being followed are so many and so various that I have no hesitation in pronouncing this bird to be a friend to humanity.

87. THE PYGMIES.

DR. G. SCHWEINFURTH,* 1870

Several days elapsed after my taking up my residence by the palace of the Monbuttoo King without my having a chance to get a view of the dwarfs, whose fame had so keenly excited my curiosity. My people, however, assured me that they had seen them. I remonstrated with them for not having secured me an opportunity of seeing for myself, and for not bringing them into contact with me. I obtained no other reply but that the dwarfs were too timid to come. After a few mornings my attention was arrested by a shouting in the camp, and I learned that Mohammed had surprised one of the Pygmies in attendance upon the King, and was conveying him, in spite of a strenuous resistance, straight to my tent. I looked up, and there, sure enough, was the strange little

* ' The Heart of Africa.'   (S. Low and Co.)

creature, perched upon Mohammed's right shoulder, nervously hugging his head, and casting glances of alarm in every direction. Mohammed soon deposited him in the seat of honour. A royal interpreter was stationed at his side. Thus, at last, was I able veritably to feast my eyes upon a living embodiment of the myths of some thousand years!

*　　　*　　　*　　　*　　　*

After a time a gentle persuasion was brought to bear, and he was induced to go through some of the characteristic evolutions of his war-dances. He was dressed, like the Monbuttoo, in a rokko-coat and plumed hat, and was armed with a miniature lance, as well as with a bow and arrow. His height I found to be about 4 feet 10 inches, and this I reckon to be the average measurement of his race.

Although I had repeatedly been astonished at witnessing the war-dances of the Niam-niam, I confess that my amazement was greater than ever when I looked upon the exhibition which the Pygmy afforded. In spite of his large, bloated belly and short bandy-legs—in spite of his age, which, by the way, was considerable—Adimokoo's agility was perfectly marvellous, and I could not help wondering whether cranes would ever be likely to contend with such creatures. The little man's leaps and attitudes were accompanied by such lively and grotesque varieties of expression that the spectators shook again and held their sides with laughter.

The interpreter explained to the Niam-niam that the Akka jump about in the grass like grasshoppers, and that they are so nimble that they shoot their arrows into an elephant's eye and drive their lances into their bellies.

*　　　*　　　*　　　*　　　*

I am not likely to forget a *rencontre* which I had with several hundred Akka warriors, and could very heartily wish that the circumstances had permitted me to give a pictorial representation of the scene. King Munza's brother Mummery, who was a kind of viceroy in the southern section of his dominions, and to whom the Akka were tributary, was just returning to the court from a successful campaign against the black Momvoo. Accompanied by a large band of soldiers, amongst whom was included a corps of Pygmies, he was conveying the bulk of the booty to his royal master. It happened on the day in question that I had been making a long excursion with my Niam-niam servants, and had heard nothing of Mummery's arrival. Towards sunset I was passing along the extensive village on my return to my quarters, when, just as I reached the wide open space in front of the royal halls, I found myself surrounded by what I conjectured must be a crowd of impudent boys, who received me with a sort of bravado fight. They pointed their arrows towards me, and behaved generally in a manner at which I could not help feeling somewhat irritated, as it betokened unwarrantable liberty and intentional disrespect. My misapprehension was soon corrected by the Niam-niam people about me. 'They are Tikkitikki,'* said they; 'you imagine that they are boys, but in truth they are men—nay, men that can fight.' At this moment a seasonable greeting from Mummery drew me off from any apprehension on my part, and from any further contemplation of the remarkable spectacle before me. In my own mind I resolved that I would minutely inspect the camp of the new-comers on the

---

* Tikkitikki is the Niam-niam designation of the Akka.

following morning, but I had reckoned without my host ; before dawn Mummery and his contingent of Pygmies had taken their departure, and thus, ' like the baseless fabric of a vision,' this people, so near and yet so unattainable, had vanished once more into the dim obscurity of the innermost continent.

NOTES.

PAGE

13. **The eighth day before the Kalends of July.** It is not clear why the English translator should make use of the Roman calendar. What Herodotus said was that the Nile begins to rise about the time of the summer solstice, June 21 of our reckoning.

14. **Winds Etesiae.** These were northerly winds, observed to blow every year, more or less, during the hot season.

16. **Syêne, a city of Thebais and Elephantina.** Thebais means the province of Thebes, the great Egyptian city, of which the famous ruins at Karnak and Luxor still remain. Syene and Elephantina were close to the First Cataract. The modern form of the name Syene is Assuan.

17. **Petronius,** Roman governor of Egypt, which became a Roman province about thirty years before Christ.

18. **4,000 stades.** The Greek stade was not far from 200 English yards.

19. **The Ptolemaic kings of Egypt.** The Ptolemies, or Greek kings of Egypt, reigned from the death of Alexander the Great, who conquered Egypt about 330 B.C., till the time of the Romans. Ptolemy Philadelphus, 285-247 B.C., was one of the most enlightened rulers known to history.
Memphis, the great city of ancient Egypt, was at a little distance from the modern Cairo.

27. **Djiza.** Now more usually spelt " Gizeh," as on p. 24.

44. **Only 1,800 feet.** It must be remembered that the rough observations of the first explorer as to altitudes and dimensions generally undergo a great deal of correction by later observers.

54. **Bahr-el-Abiad,** the White Nile.

55. **Bahr-el-Gebel,** the Nile above the junction of the Bahr-al-Ghazal.

60. **Kaffiés.** Caravans.

61. **Shrab.** The word now generally used to describe this appearance is " mirage."

PAGE

72. **Women on the sea-coast.** The Moslem women of Northern Africa, who veil their faces.

82. **Addressed me in Turkish.** Barth was representing himself as a Turkish merchant.

87. **Libya.** This word was used by the ancients much as "Africa" is with us.

87. **Pillars of Hercules.** This is the ancient name for the Straits of Gibraltar. The rock of Gibraltar was the northern pillar.

91. **The said river.** The Rio Grande.

92. **Almadias,** canoes.

95. **Diego Cam, 1484.** The exact year of the discovery is matter of dispute.

97. **Though they steered thus for several days, they did not strike land.** They had, in fact, got to the south of the Cape of Good Hope, which they did not see until they passed it on the return journey (p. 99).

108. **King John II.,** at the end of the fifteenth century.

109. **A king's stranger.** The word "neguz," nowadays spelt "Negus," means "king" in Abyssinian.

112. **Sistrum,** a rattle.

118. **The promontory named Soloes.** Soloes, or Soloeis (p. 88), is considered to be the modern Cape Cantin.

119. **Tombuto,** Timbuctoo.

120. **Prete Gianni,** Prester John.

122. **With concern.** Mungo Park perceived that, as it soon proved, he would no longer be able to pass for a Moor himself.

127 **The Benin River.** This extract, included in Bosman's famous work on "Guinea," is from a letter written to Bosman by a correspondent named Nyendael. Bosman was chief factor of the Dutch settlement at Elmina.

137. **The Quorra,** the main stream of the Niger.

142. **Tobes.** *Cf.* p. 73.

149. **The Boers.** Boer, or Boor, as it was often written, merely means a farmer.
    A. Sparrman. Sparrman, like Horneman (p. 68), was a Swede.

150. **Tyger-berg.** To the Cape Colonist a "tiger" means a leopard, a "wolf" (p. 154), a hyena.

155. **Tribulus terrestris,** a prickly plant, on which Sparrman had sat down.

161. **Boshies-men,** now spelt "Bosjesmen," the Dutch form of the word "Bushmen."

166. **This antelope drinks every day.** Many African antelopes can go a very long time without drinking, or apparently even desiring to drink.

168. **Portugalls,** Portuguese. **Kafars,** Kaffirs.
    Cuama, the River Zambesi.

169. **Truck,** traffic.

171. **Menhirs,** "long-stones" set up on end.

188. **In the elevation of 5 degrees.** Where the south pole is 5° above the horizon, or latitude 5° south.

PAGE
189. **Bansas**, native villages.
190. **Embomma**. This place (*cf.* p. 204) is now written " Boma."
195 **Ujiji**, on the eastern shore of Lake Tanganyika.
196. **Gondokoro**. This place is on the Upper Nile, but below the Lake Albert Nyanza, by which Livingstone had supposed the Lualaba to join the Nile.
197. **Katombéla**. This place will not easily be found on the map, but it is close to the Portuguese town of Benguela.
201. **Tippoo-Tib**, the famous Arab slave-trader.
206. **Frank**, Frank Pocock, Stanley's only white companion on this journey, who was drowned in the Congo.
212. **Cordova**, site of the famous Moorish university.
214. **Bononia**, Bologna.
      Azaphi, Saffi.
217. **Mihrab**, a niche in the wall of a mosque, indicating the direction of the sacred city, Mecca.
232. **St. Paul**. St. Paul de Loanda, the capital of Angola. Andrew Battel, after a long captivity among the Portuguese, and many wanderings in the wilds of West Africa, got safely back to his home in Essex.
234. **With two little Sticks**, by rubbing two pieces of wood together.
237. **Anacondas**, a large kind of boa-constrictor.
      Epiphytes, plants which have no root in the ground, but grow upon other plants.
239. **Abattis**, a fortification made of the branches of trees.
248. **Mkaranga**, an inhabitant of Ukaranga.
      Upas-tree, the fabled upas-tree of Java, which poisoned all that came near it.
249. **Suliman ibn Daood**, Solomon, the son of David, who in Arabic tradition is the greatest of all magicians.
251. **Bandoleer**, a leathern case attached to a belt.

THE END.

BILLING AND SONS, PRINTERS, GUILDFORD.

www.ingramcontent.com/pod-product-compliance
Lightning Source LLC
Chambersburg PA
CBHW030351270326
41926CB00009B/1047